D0416848

A Corner of Paradise

Also by Peter Davies

Mare's Milk and Wild Honey

A
Corner of
Paradise

Peter Davies

**With drawings by
Sandra Oakins**

André Deutsch

First published in 1992
by André Deutsch Limited
105-106 Great Russell Street
London WC1B 3LJ

Text copyright © 1992 by Peter Davies
Illustrations copyright © 1992 by Sandra Oakins

British Library Cataloguing in Publication Data
Davies, Peter, *1928-*
    A corner of paradise.
    I. Title
    942.454

ISBN 0–233–98765–7

Printed in Great Britain by
WBC, Bridgend

To my brother, John

Three lives hath one life —
Iron, honey, gold.
The gold, the honey gone —
Left is the hard and cold.

Isaac Rosenberg

Contents

In the Merry Month of May

It was bright May. The horse chestnuts were in flower;
the lilac too. My father was sitting on a stone outside
the fold gate – a kind of mounting block – when I came
home from school. He was reliving the battles of the
war – his war, 1914 to '18. Gyp, our old greyhound,
was lying flat at his feet – so flat he was almost two-
dimensional. He was not listening. He had heard it all
a thousand times before. He had his own campaigns to
dream about: 'going over the top . . . ' Only he was in
pursuit of hares, not Huns.

'Old faithfuls never die,' my father crooned: a new
variation on an old ground bass. He nudged the dog's
backside with his foot and smiled at me. It was a mystery to me how my father, who smoked continuously,
could talk and joke and laugh and croon and cough
without dislodging his cigarette from his half-closed

lips. Sometimes there was a spillage of ash, but that he would gently dust with a long-fingered hand from his thigh. He was a gentle man really, especially in his relations with animals.

Gyp was not his dog. He belonged to my elder brother, John, who had paid the gypsies five shillings for him – and thrown in one of my father's Woodbine cigarettes. That was when Gyp was about a month or six weeks old, a milky ball of white and blue-grey puppy flesh. He slept and twitched between meals for days. 'He's growing in his sleep,' we were told. And so he lengthened like a piece of string, his long legs stretched out fore and aft. Now he was twelve; his haunch pins showed like tent-pegs through his skin; and, like my father, he had grown more grey with age.

My father's cap was tilted upwards to the sun. His cigarette burned grey between his lips. His cap and his cigarette were both barometers by which I read his moods. Tilted up, the former said 'set fair'; drawn down over his eyes, it meant 'look out!' Likewise a sudden brilliance in the latter, even in bright sunshine, meant 'jump to it, my lad – and quick!'

Inside the house, my mother was swinging a steaming floor-cloth in a wide arc over the shining cardinal red tiles of the kitchen floor. The tiles grew cloudy as they dried, and so did the smile on Mother's face. The veins protruded from her arms. She gave the cloth a final twist.

'There, that'll do for today,' she said, and staggered to her feet. She always washed the floor that way, down on her hands and knees.

It would not do for today, of course. There was still the tea to get, and the washing up to do, and some ironing perhaps, or socks to darn, or trousers to patch and buttons to sew on shirts. But washing the floor marked the end of the dirtier part of the day, and – it being Friday – the dirtier part of the week.

'If you can only remember to wipe your feet on the bag outside,' she said.

On Fridays Mother washed the sacks as well, and placed one, clean and dry, by the back door to stop us bringing pig- and cow-muck into the house.

'And kindly take this bran-mash off the fire, I want to get the tea.'

A bran-mash coughed and bubbled in a smoke-blackened bucket on the hob above the kitchen fire. It was the universal cure for sick animals; with a little linseed oil, it would put a calved-down cow back on her feet. It was as common a feature of our living room hearth as a perforated shoe-box in which might be, swaddled in pink flannel, a whistling piglet or a handful of cheeping chicks.

'Dickie's coming later,' I said, hoisting the bran-mash out of the way.

'Oh, I don't mind him,' she said, tidying her still-dark hair. Something in Mother was indestructible.

'Can he stay the night?'

'He usually does.'

'OK, I'll take the bran-mash and—'

'Bring me some beastings when you've changed and done the milking. I'll make a beastings pie.'

Beastings was the first strong milk from a cow after she had calved. It was too thick, pink and creamy to send to the dairy, but it made wonderful pies. Dickie might never have had beastings pie.

He was one of my friends from Shrewsbury who came regularly: cultured sophisticates, drawn as it were by a magnet to our little holding in the wilderness – beastings pies, pork pies, rabbit pies and all. We had no running water, no electricity, no telephone, no sanitation at Little Ness. But we had strong meat and laughter. I had two beautiful sisters. And it was Maytime; it was lily of the valley time; it was cuckoo time and cowslip time; it was roaring dandelion time. It was the time of the singing of birds when the voice of the turtle was heard in our land.

My father took the bran-mash from me at the cow-house door.

'Mustn't give it 'er 'ot,' he said.

'Is it a heifer?' I asked, meaning the calf.

'A bull,' he said. 'A big un, too.'

'We'll have to sell him, then,' I said unquestioningly. All my hopes of Anna, our young Friesian, having a young Anna to breed from were dashed. The cow had dropped her cleansing in shining, sickening-smelling sheaths of blood and water, in the channel behind her. A skein of membrane still hung by her tail. It flashed in a shaft of light from the door. The calf was making bull-headed attempts to find his mother's milk somewhere between her front legs.

'She's got a good bag,' I said.

'Tight as a drum.' My father coughed and ash fell into the mash. 'Unded, see. I'll put this in 'er boosey in a minute. Then put the calf in the calf-kit. 'Er'll bellock all night,' he said – meaning the cow. He looked disdainfully at my school clothes.

'I'll go and change,' I said, and fled the scene.

I was quicker than usual getting into my working clothes. I wanted to shift the afterbirth, the cleansing as we called it, before Dickie came. He would not be much impressed by that.

'What's a boosey?' he would ask, watching me milk in the morning.

'The manger,' I would say. 'Away in a boosey, no crib for a bed . . . '

'What's unded?'

'Oh, unded means sore, distended, tight as a drum,' I would add, stylishly drawing more beastings, booming down into the pail.

Unded and bellock and boosey and calf-kit were

all words which we used at Little Ness, as peculiar to home as detention and swot and crib were to school. Two worlds apart.

It was the tensions and contrasts between those two worlds – two unlike poles – that attracted our town friends to Little Ness, I supposed. It was the tensions and contrasts between our parents that electrified the atmosphere at home and made us children what we were.

I threw my school clothes down on the bed, happy to shed them for another weekend.

It was May when we first came to Little Ness, fourteen years before, when I was three. The grass was ankle high between the cobblestones in the big yard – grass which we four children were to spend our lives, it seemed, digging out with old bone-handled kitchen knives. Our knees knew the imprint of those stones as well as they knew that of the coconut matting which we knelt on in church. 'From grass and long litanies, good Lord deliver us,' we prayed.

High cliffs of hay remained invitingly in the barn. My older brother and I were up and away. We quickly found the warm pigsties, sandstone-walled like everything here, and walked all over them. We found the woodplace, subterranean and dim, and then the dark, damp-smelling passages, cobweb-festooned, that led round the back of the furnace-hole, for our new home was a disused malthouse. We stumbled on dozens of bottles, squeaking and squirting from under our feet. I put one to my innocent lips and drained it. It was the foulest stuff imaginable. It gave me a distaste for beer and a fear of the dark. I could never, even now that I was seventeen, show anyone round that furnace-hole – or the cellar beneath the stairs in the house. I was still afraid to pass the cellar door with

13

my candle flickering in the draught of a raw winter's night.

'You live in a corner of paradise,' said Dickie when he came that lovely May evening in 1946. 'A place where time has stood still.'

'A corner of paradise from which the devil has not been thrown out,' I shrugged. 'We keep him at bay.'

'That's what I like about it,' he smiled handsomely. I knew what he meant; but, being secretly ashamed of the darkness in our lives, I tried to show him all that was light.

Where else would he see a new-born Friesian calf? Or the jewelled and braided plumage of a pair of fan-tailed turtle doves performing their courtly aerial dance in silvery evening light?

'That's why Aunt Alice comes at Easter,' I said. 'To see the daffodils. Only she missed them this year. Easter was late.' We laughed.

'She still gives me a Saturday penny when she comes,' I added. 'Even though she really looks down on me, thinks I'm not given to books – a rural roughneck! Come on. Race you to the Mound!'

I led him up to the Mound, the domed tumulus that rose, crowned with a dark yew tree, beside our ancient sandstone church. It was, it seemed, a pagan 'green hill', standing there outside the Christian sandstone city wall.

'Cynddylan's grave,' said Dickie. His mother being Welsh, he was able to give the Celtic warrior prince the honour due to his name.

'Yes,' I said, sitting down, 'it's strange to think that the last Welsh Lord of Pengwern Powys may have received a hurried and blood-stained burial here.' The words came pat off the page of the Reverend P. A. Parrott's book.

'In this peaceful place,' said Dickie, chewing a piece of grass.

'And the chapel was probably built in the reign

14

of King Stephen as a protection for the poor, and out of regard to the warlike troubles of the time,' I said, remembering more of our scholarly vicar's words, and pleased with the effect.

We looked across to the clear South Shropshire hills: a shoulder of Caer Caradoc, the long tail of the Stiperstones, the Callow surmounted with trees that looked like one of our stackyard staddlestones, and Pontesford Hill that looked like a maned lion lying down. Then, squinting into the setting sun, we picked out the helmed head of the Breidden, battle-bruised.

'Where's Nesscliff Hill then?' Dickie asked.

'Drowning in the blood-red rays of the sun,' I said. 'The central battleground of all the struggles in the history of these parts.' The words came straight off the page of the Reverend F. Brighton's book about Great Ness.

'And the Cliffe?'

'Beyond the school, down Valeswood Lane.'

Standing up and peering through more yew trees shadowing the church and overhanging its encircling wall, we could just see the Cliffe, a low heath like a small brother of the more famous and romantic Nesscliff Hill.

'And what's this lane?' asked Dickie, pointing to the road that ran behind the church.

'It goes to World's End,' I said.

'It does indeed,' he said.

We ranged around the churchyard, sitting down for a while on the grass by my grandparents' grave. There you could see all the lands that had once been theirs – fertile and well-stocked, bordering the River Perry: as fine a sight as any you could wish to see. It hurt me that my father did not share this view, he who had gone from here when he was seventeen to fight for the King!

15

But he sat looking west, to the eternally unhelpful hills.

'Where's Laura?' Dickie asked suddenly. Like everyone else, he had always liked my twin sister.

'In the Land Army. Comes home some weekends.'

'Busman's holiday,' he smiled. 'And Belle?'

'Gone to the Young Farmers' Club.'

'Pity,' he said, looking as if he meant it. Then, after a pause, 'You're a dreamer,' he said, teasing my chin with a bent of grass. 'Where do you get it from?'

'Dreaminess – and good looks, from my father,' I said. I meant it too.

'And from your mum?'

'A certain Christian savagery!' I spat out a piece of grass. 'And the gleam of hope in the tail of her eye.'

'Meaning?' he asked.

'Well, she's up and doing, and she sings at her work – "South of the Border" one minute, and away with *The Chocolate Soldier* or *The Student Prince* the next. Dad only sits around and sings "Old Soldiers Never Die".' I shrugged and, standing up, I felt a sudden chill.

'You're like a little band against the world,' he said.

'But the band is breaking up,' I said.

'What will you do?' he asked.

'Dunno.'

Just then the Chesneys, Vic and Bob, roared past in an MG sports, towels flapping out of the dicky at the back. Miracle boys with bikes, they were now miracle men with cars.

'They've been to the river,' I said. 'I might go with them at Whit.'

'Swimming? In the river?' said Dickie, and seemed quite shocked at the thought.

'We could go tomorrow,' said I.

'I can't,' he said quickly. 'ATC parade in the morning and cricket at Cound in the afternoon.'

'And on Sunday?'

'Church, I suppose.'

16

'Psalm singing can put years on you,' I said mockingly. 'Fearfulness and trembling are come upon me, and an horrible dread hath overwhelmed me,' I cantorized.

'Oh my God, I cry in the daytime, and in the night season also I take no rest,' he responded, *à la* decani.

A tawny owl flew out of an old yew tree, so hollow that the sexton had put a door on it and used it as a shed in which to keep his tools.

'What's in there then?' asked Dickie, knocking on the door, as if expecting a supernatural reply.

'Sexton's lean, long-handled tool . . . '

I laughed, and ran down the hill for home. I could never outrun Dickie, and on this occasion I caught my foot in a rabbit hole – the shallow sort that rabbits make in spring. I fell headlong. He fell after me, and we wrestled on the ground, biting one another's ears and clouding our clothes in dusty earth.

'I'll get it in the ear when I get home!'

'Whistle britches,' he said, clouting my corded derrière to brush me down.

'Sansculotte,' I spluttered back, and snatched his belt.

Blowing with pain and laughter, we tidied up our shirts.

A Spitfire flew low out of the west. We could see the pilot in the cockpit and read the number on the fuselage.

'He's late going home,' said Dickie.

'To Tern Hill,' I guessed.

'I'll fly one of them, one day!' His face was transfigured at the thought.

'But not till next year,' I hoped against hope.

'No. Have to get a place at Cambridge first.' His Latin eyes looked bright.

This excitement, and Dickie's always engaging manner,

probably saved me from a drubbing when we got inside the house.

'You look like one of the ruins that Cromwell knocked about a bit,' my mother said.

'Old Ironsides,' I said, indicating Dickie, who looked cool and self-possessed as ever.

Only country boys go red in the face, I thought, looking at myself in the mirror. Only country boys are ticklish, I thought, examining a swollen bottom lip.

It was not so bad that it stopped me eating my supper or tackling Dickie again in bed.

We heard my mother cough and smelt her cigarette as she stepped slowly up the stairs: she always smoked and read in bed. We heard my sister Belle tiptoeing after her. But not my father's heavy tread.

We talked for hours that night, mainly about what we would do to make the most of the time we had left. What a programme he had set himself, the fellow! He was in the classical sixth at school, captain of cricket and a flight sergeant in the ATC. He had won the steeplechase. He played the violin. His voice had broken properly, unlike mine, so he could still sing in the choir. He was heading for the RAF, and Cambridge after that.

'I'm going to get an MG,' I said. But he, ahead of me again, was fast asleep.

Intemperate June

I was lying on the lawn on a juicy June day. I had been lying there over half an hour. My mother told me so when she and my younger sister Belle sailed down the garden path in summer hats to catch the two o'clock bus to town.

'Keep the gate shut,' my mother said. 'And cut the grass.' Those were her last words. They were usually her last words.

Women always wanted things cutting: toenails, fingernails, grass and hair. Men didn't mind so much. But women did. 'Get your hair cut!'

Mine was just nice and long. I could almost touch my forelock with my tongue as I lay there in the grass. It tasted a bit like old hay.

Yes, women had this thing about grass. They just wouldn't let it grow. It had to be dug out from between the cobblestones with a knife; it had to be clipped, if it was the lawn, with a pair of shears (this was before we got our new Qualcast lawn-mower).

'You'd do better with a pair of scissors,' said the

next-door's cowman, waggishly waving a stick and beating it on the handlebars of his bike as he rode behind the cows. But now we had a proper push-mower. It sent the grass flying like green sparks into the shimmering air. It ticked and trilled like a chatter-box when you turned it over and trailed it backwards down the path. Lift it up sharply, and it spun like a Hornby train. It wasn't perfect – the box didn't really fit – but Mrs Garry's daughter from the post office borrowed it once a fortnight, carrying it single-handed up the village with as little effort as she swung the washing out. Once a year would have been enough for me.

I would make all grass into hay, like our front field. Let it alone: that, it seemed to me, was a man's way. Our hay, for instance, you weren't allowed to go near while it was being drawn, and we 'drew' it all through the spring. From the front bedroom windows we could see the days lengthening with the hay; and watch the sun take longer to go down behind the western hills. It set just over the Breiddens, silvering the Severn at Melverley and Montford Bridge and all the hayfields in between – soft seas of summer-scented hay . . .

But no, women must have their grass all neatly cut. No bents for ladybirds to climb. No blades to press between your thumbs and blow at, making a ripping noise such as a mare makes when she opens her hocks and lifts her tail. No slender juicy stalks to suck that made your teeth go green. The one I was sucking was sweet; but, yes, my teeth were not the purest white. I'd better stop . . . Farmer's lung – one old chap in the village had died from it; but that was from straw. I never could understand why anyone sucked straw.

Kite chewed grass. Kite who had interested me in Dracula between movements of the field in cricket matches. An elegant dreamer, he had the monumental idleness of a horse and never felt inclined to stop – or

20

start – a run! He looked like Rupert Brooke: a flaxen
Saxon with grey, far-seeing eyes. He kept promising
that one day he would come out to Little Ness, but
he never did.

A fly landed on my arm. 'Flies feed on every
kind of filth,' our science master used to say, with
deadly emphasis. Short-haired and long-armed was
Jock, long gone to the war. He said grass with a very
short a, so clipped that it made his moustache bristle.
He could knock you from one side of the classroom to
the other. He would not have said 'the grass'. He would
have said 'the grasses'. There were so many: Timothy,
Fescue, Crested Dog's Tail, Couch or Twitch (which
we called Squitch), Sweet Vernal Grass – such lovely
names! I went looking for them in our hay and got my
backside kicked for my pains. I could only see bents in
our lawn, the sort you twirled in a girl's hair and pulled
to make her cry 'Ouch!' That was why women wanted
grass cut!

My twin sister Laura came out.

'You're supposed to cut the grass, not roll in it,'
she said.

'I like rolling in it,' I said, and turned over to search
for more bents and ladybirds. The sun was almost too
much for me. I thought I would have to go in – or move
over to the lilac hedge. The grass grew longer, cooler,
greener there. Not so sweet perhaps, but you couldn't
have everything. There was no privacy on our lawn,
no trees giving shade. Not like Little Ness House where
low branches of cedar trees swept down like peacocks'
tails on acres of green baize, where Alf Yeomans kept
the gardens like the grounds of Buckingham Palace. Mrs
Darby was the old Squire's wife. She didn't say grass;
she said grahs, the way Mr Parrott, our parson, said
pahs – and his neighbour's ahs . . . We Shropshire-ites
said ass both for donkey and bum. And we said gay-t,
for gate, and buz for bus . . .

21

Lucky for me my mum 'ad ketched the buz. I shudna bin lyin' 'ere if 'er adna! I laughed to my guilty self.

Two people particularly made me feel guilty: Aunt Alice and my brother John. The latter, though only seventeen months older than I, was so far ahead of me academically he had got clean away. He and Aunt Alice appeared as ghosts in the window of the Empty Room which overlooked our lawn. Their silence was rebuke enough.

Aunt Alice's spirit was everywhere in the Empty Room. A large spare room, where originally we kept only the piano, she had filled it with her furniture, her moth-balls and her books. Dyspeptic and pince-nezed, with hair drawn up like an onion-dome on her head, she was my mother's maiden aunt – her only remaining relative, in fact. She had yellow, bulbous eyes, a yellow tongue and yellow teeth. She dressed herself in brown, wore sensible shoes, and led a literary and nomadic life. She walked about our lanes and spoke to me of the moaning of doves in immemorial elms, the short and simple annals of the poor, the quiet desperation of their lives. At seventeen it amused me to think that she, who quoted Lewis Carroll and Tennyson, was born before Father William and conceived before the Lady of Shalott.

She had money; we knew she had money; but we did not know how much. Her father, Peter Cowell, was an important man in Liverpool: the Chief City Librarian. Her brother, Percy, had made – and lost – fortunes on the floor of the Cotton Exchange. A Wicked Uncle! we rejoiced. Any children?

'No children – only chorus girls,' Mother said darkly, disappointedly.

Alice's other brother, Alfred, was our mother's father. He was 'given to music'. A noted church organist, he had conceived Mother, as it were, between voluntaries. He seems to have regarded her birth as the cause of his wife's death. Expected to give the child a name, he expended little effort or time on that: the three letters of the name of the month in which she was born would do. May.

Aunt Alice's other name was Petrina, after her father. Imagine. With money and a name like that she might have traded in cottons, as Marco Polo traded in silks. She might have gone east to the Court of the Khedive or the King of Siam. Instead she went west, to Devon; but her next stop, after visiting us, was usually Evesham (the Vale) where the asparagus was 'more advanced' and the rabbits 'ungovernable'.

More startling than Aunt Alice's, was the ghost of John when it appeared, towelled like a prophet, head bent over the calculus. He had spent the past two years at Birmingham University studying maths: $E = mc^2$! But I still saw him as I did when he was at home: a towel like a cold-water bandage wrapped round his head.

'You're only reading H.G. Wells with a brown-paper cover on!' I shouted to show how shrewd I was.

'I'm the Invisible Man,' he yelled, hurling an imaginary javelin at me, for the second time that day. 'Find something to do – like a French unseen!'

I could not emulate John, so I had put science and maths behind me and embraced the siren charms of the arts: History (the Bourbons), French, and English literature (Keats). I was also aiming to be a concert pianist. I really thought I could be as good as Paderewski by the time I got to his age . . . Pachmann, Pouishnoff, they were all old. I specialized in pieces that were very loud and very fast. My father had threatened to break up the piano with an axe; he didn't want even a retired Pachmann in the house. But my father was more often than not at the pub – or

23

used to be when he still had the black pony, Dorothy
May . . .

What had happened to Dorothy May? – she of
the six senses and second sight, who was always
old. Had she, like Elijah, been taken up into heaven
in a whirlwind? Had she, like those other people in
the Bible, Moses & Co., been destined never to see
death? Or had she been taken away one day when my
sisters and I were at school, by Price's of Hordley, the
knackermen? We never asked. She was just not there
any more, like the old Kelsall cow: her time had come.
She was not there any more in the Top Field with
Topsy, my little Welsh mountain pony, mischievously
mumbling between mouthfuls or undoing the plaits and
straightening out each other's manes . . .

We shunned death on our farm – death and procre-
ation. They were all around us. They stalked the fields
and skirted the hedgerows. They hid in the barns. They
sometimes stared us in the face. We shut our eyes or
walked by on the other side.

Since we had lost Dorothy May I did not have
to milk so often at night. Dad could not get to the
pub, unless someone gave him a lift. He might still
be drunk after last night; still asleep in the barn. We
never knew. It was sometimes better not to try to find
out.

I survived by keeping my head down, as a Berk-
shire parson reported he had done in the Civil War
. . . I liked History. I liked the extravagance of the
ancien régime and the splendour of the Sun King's
court at Versailles. 'Things will last my lifetime' – I
agreed with Louis XIV, I did not want change. Look
how revolution had affected Chopin: Chopin had long
hair. And when did his mother last cut his fingernails?
I would have to practise. But not now . . .

There were three hours before milking would have
to begin, and another two before the reckoning would

24

be made on my lawn-mowing. John Vagg's bus would
leave Shrewsbury at a quarter to eight as it had for years
with my mother running to catch it after seeing *Spring
in Park Lane* or *Love on the Dole*, sad or starry-eyed, but
ready to face cold comfort for another week. It would
pass through Bicton village, non-stop; descend Grange
Bank to Montford Bridge; and then its deviations would
begin. From Forton to Fitz was one long crawl; and
thence to Grafton and Nibs Heath, to Little Ness and
Valeswood, on to Knockin Heath or Nescliff. There
were two depots where Vagg's buses, red-green drag-
ons, holed up in sandy hollows for the night; then came
nosing out of Valeswood to breathe fire and light along
our lanes each Saturday – or on weekdays to snatch
up other groups of Priory schoolboys trembling with
their homework only half-done all along the A5 road;
at Great Ness, Ensdon, Shrawardine and us at Montford
Bridge. Mad Jack and Spen drove us at speed – no time
to think of ablatives. A slow declension into the old
borough of Frankwell, the dragon sometimes sizzling
through a flood . . . But on Saturdays John, who sang
'Killarney' and 'The Way You Look Tonight', deposited
all the dames of the district at their doors. He helped
them with their market baskets which they had earlier
taken into Shrewsbury laden with the produce of the
country, which were now still heavier with the produce
of the town: tins of peaches, and packets of blancmange,
and slabs of cherry cake for Sunday tea . . .

My father would say: 'Any more for billy-mange,'
which would be white and trembling under the weight
of his strong arm. When I went to Dickie's for tea
they had pink blancmange, but ours in the country
was white, as it should be: *blanc mange*, you see.
Louis Quatorze would have understood that. '*Après
moi le blancmange*,' he would have said.' I rolled my
tongue round the words as I rolled another stem of
grass between my thumbs and forefingers, practising

25

for the time when I would roll my own cigarettes. Smoking gave you bad breath, but it was manly to roll your own . . .

A trickle of sweat ran down the channel in my hollow chest and swilled around my waist. My shirt was open. I could see the little River Perrys running round my wrinkled ribs and flowing on to join the Severn below. I was already smelling like a lawn-mower, and would have to go and wash. 'Finished the lawn then?' my watchful sister would say. I would put my sweaty shirt back on over my body, rainwater wet, and go and call up the cud-chewing cows.

'What lawn?' I would ask.

'The one you've been rolling on,' she would say. And I would say, Rolling is good for grass; adding, sotto voce, that grass is good for rolling on . . .

I would have taken my shirt off there and then, but it was not quite done to show your tin ribs and expose your guilt so completely. Naked idleness was next to godlessness. So I covered myself up with a fig-leaf, metaphorically, and felt ashamed, like Adam and Eve.

So that's why women wanted the grass cut! They were always on the lookout for the serpent. God (who was a man) did not have the grass cut; so Eve failed to see the serpent, sinuous as the wind in the hay, approaching. And even when she saw it she did not know how to deal with it. Adam would have knocked it on the head with a stick . . . Grass is a cover for sin, so keep it short.

Yes, grass is a cover for sin, I thought: under the hedges, long, yielding, good cover for courting couples – especially soldiers from Nescliff camp with their khaki greatcoats for camouflage . . . What a lovely word was camouflage! Get a greatcoat . . . Roll your own . . . Something other than sweat . . .

Gyp sidled onto the lawn, nuzzled under my arm and licked my face.

'Shake hands, Gyp,' I said – a thing he almost scorned to do, as if he could not stoop so low. His body, which had always been like a coiled spring, had gradually unwound, gone slack. His teeth were yellow and worn, his muzzle mealy-grey, his one eye filmed with blue as with a milky cloud. His breath was not so sweet, but I did not object. He was our venerable Gyp; we revered him. He had a neck like a swan, a head like a drake, a chest like a barrel and a tail like a snake. He could still pick up a young rabbit and hand it to you as if it were a lady's glove. He had outlasted all our older pets: our first bantams, my little pink pig, John's stinking billy-goat.

Seeing the King would not be going a-hunting today, he accepted the situation like an amiable old courtier, yawned and stretched out at my feet. He lay full-length, as he did when he was a puppy, his hind legs trailing like a swan in flight.

Just then I heard a slither of hooves on the cobble-stones in the yard, the fold gate closing with a bang, a skirmish of hooves on the road past the front of the house, and, most alarming to me, I caught the smell of cigarette smoke hanging in the air.

'Where are you going?' I hollered after my father, who was disappearing, legs dangling, down the road on my pony's back. No answer.

I knew where he was going. He was going to the hotel in Nesscliff to get drunk. Afternoon, or no afternoon, he would go round the back. I must stop him, not for his sake, but Topsy's. I would run through the Front Field, hay or no hay, into the Cow Lane and cut him off. I had never seen my father on horseback before. There was an old photograph of him in the Yeomanry: smart, sober and seventeen. And Little Ness was full of echoes of the days when he and his five brothers, like all farm lads, showed off on their 'tits', as we, in our generation, showed off on our bikes. He taught me to ride: walk, trot, canter, walk again and stop, collectedly. His concern was always for the horse; in my case, this brave little pony of under twelve hands. I called her mine, but she really belonged and answered to him. All ponies answered to him. And there was talk of how he rode Topsy round the yard of the Big House when John became the first in our family to win a scholarship to the Priory School: a re-enactment, perhaps, of his own graduation in horsemanship when he was a boy, and the Big House was his home. The yard at the old malthouse (Church House, as it was now known) would have been too small.

Too small! My pony was too small, and fifteen years old. And white with age. My father was over six feet tall, and fourteen stone. His feet trailed on the ground.

I struggled through the hay. Thistles hung on to my trousers and nettles stung through to my thighs. Even the whispering grasses formed knots and snagged themselves around my knees. A startled partridge whirred its wings, creaked like an un-oiled gate, and planed down into the lane. I followed it. Nothing startled Topsy, but she had the wild eye and arched neck of the horses in those stained-glass windows in our church depicting the warrior saints. Her tail was up. And, for all the incongruity of size, my father rode with a stately firmness and the faded elegance of King Lear. His cigarette brightened under the buckled peak of his cap.

'Get off!' I gasped. He clicked his tongue and kept to his course. 'You're too heavy!' I shouted. 'You'll break her back!' But I knew this wasn't true. Topsy had carried my brother and me together.

Then I thought of the traffic on the Holyhead road. 'The traffic,' I shouted. 'You'll kill her. You'll have an accident. It isn't fair!' I picked up a stick and threw it, missing so wildly I felt both shame and relief.

28

There was a gate across the lane a hundred yards ahead where he would have to dismount. I would tackle him there. But Topsy was one of those ponies, skilled at opening gates themselves, that go right up to them, not stopping short or stepping back, and my father, equally skilled, had no need to dismount.

My blood was up. I was Hotspur and Prince Hal rolled into one, I would challenge the old king's right to the throne: the young cock versus the old.

I went for his cap. With one swing of my hasty arm I knocked it off. And his cigarette, which, like the cap, my father never went out without, went with it in a shower of sparks. The pony suddenly swinging round, my father slumped to the ground, as if all his strength had been in his cap and his cigarette.

I left him there and took the pony home. My mind went back to the time I had tapped an angry cockerel on the head with the fowlhouse key – I thought I had killed him.

I thought I had killed my father. But I was so blind with anger, I thought only of the pony and returning her safely to the field. I prayed that Laura would not be about. I would get on with the milking, not stopping for tea.

I did not ride Topsy. Just led her, my hand on her sweating withers, back to the field. Freed from the bridle, she always shook herself vigorously, snorted, took a few prancing steps with her head and tail held high, shook herself again and resumed grazing where she had left off, as if nothing had happened.

Laura called me for tea. Was it that late already?

'I can't come yet. Got to milk!'

At this time of year, when grass was plentiful and milk was cheap, we had two shippons full of high-yielding new-milch cows. We never had so many in November when milk was dear. It would take two hours.

'Cow-up! Cow-up!' The sleek-coated, wide-uddered cows slopped water from the drinking trough we filled by hand from the pump, and dunged the yard.

I tied them up mechanically; their pecking order was as well observed by us as by them. No sooner was my foaming pail emptied than it was full again. I loved the sound of milk stroked into the pail with a full head on it. It was like a baby breathing in its sleep. When you started again, drumming on the bottom of the pail, it was like arrows landing on a target of tin. Ping! Then purr again. The pail filled up. Milk prattles as it settles in the pail. And milkers talk to themselves. And occasionally to the cows. 'Ho, me ol' beauty . . . Hold y'up, ya so-an'-so!'

I'd filled two churns. I'd finished the first shippon and let the cows out. I went to begin the second, usually harder. The cows having finished their cake, they did not let their milk down so well; they stood more awkwardly.

'Move over,' I said to one. 'Get up,' I said to the next, who was lying down and losing her milk on the floor. A third stood back in the channel as if any old time would do, and kicked dung onto her newly washed teats. I went for a cup of tea.

Five minutes later I was pinging away on the bottom of my bucket when I heard a cough. Well, cows do cough sometimes. I prattled on. I reached the whispering stage where bubbles swell and breathe awhile and die . . . And then I heard the cough again. It was my father quietly milking away at the far end of the shippon, cap in place as usual, with the crazy peak at the back, and his cigarette burnt right down to his lips.

Relieved, I slunk back to the lawn. Sweat pricking in my temples, grass flying everywhere, I swung the

30

mower in a frenzy – leaving off the box to add speed to the task.

The parson went by unsmiling – a black soul in black, shining shoes.

The gold, the honey gone

Whitsuntide was late that year – and more than usually promising. For spring came haltingly to Little Ness. Easter was always cold. Winter returned when the blackthorn bloomed; when we usually killed the pig; and the old pear tree dropped fresh tears like bubbles of milk on the cobblestones outside the house. There might be a lull and soft airs for a week or two, but then the north wind would come out of Ruyton and blast the plum trees in our orchard, scattering snow-like petals along with Mother's washing far and wide. 'Plum winter' we called that.

No wonder we set so much store by Whit. Then, with any luck, we would bathe in the river; then, because it was half-term, we would forget about school, unseens and mock exams; then lilac fountained, laburnum blazed, poppies and paeonies flamed, flattened and fell; the cool wild rose appeared – my favourite flower, God's masterpiece, whose subtle scent and smile He knew I never could resist. Then we might see a purple

emperor, a lesser spotted woodpecker, a young fox
tenderfooting it across the Cow Lane field, skimming
the cowslips as he went; then we might have potatoes
fresh from the garden, and early peas with English
lamb, and, afterwards, the first pink shoots of rhubarb
in a pie.

Then Lucy and Jim, our old neighbours at Wigmarsh,
would come – no doubt about that. Well-fed, we'd walk
between the ruminating cows and Jim would bless them
with a laying on of hands. Nothing delighted me more
than this ceremony of his: the blessing of the cows.
'Well, fancy,' he would say. 'Still got Gyp. Still got
the little white pony, too.' Deep in daisies we would
dream, collecting buttercup gold-dust on our Sunday
shining shoes. Nothing was so white as Whit – except it
were our hopes – and nothing so golden as then, except
it were our dreams. We almost spake with tongues . . .

'John writes to say he's coming home for Whit,' my
mother sang. That was on the Saturday. 'He doesn't
give me much notice.'

She was wrestling with torn newspapers and paraffin,
trying to relight the fire.

'Smoke gets in your eyes,' she said with half a
laugh and half a tear. 'I've got to get some baking
done.'

When Mother descended to the use of gots and gets
it was indeed a sign that time was running out. She
pointed to the letter propped up by a jam kettle on the
mantelpiece – the one that held my father's cigarettes;
it was fuller than usual at the end of the week.

I did not read the letter then. I had only just finished the milking. Breakfast would be late. We would
be behind all day.

'Someone to help you with the milking,' Mother
said.

He'll get me a ride in the Chesneys' MG, I thought,
and went outside again. He, John, had probably finished

his exams, I thought. But he'd only been back a few weeks.

I turned the cattle out, swept up, wrote the labels for the milk churns, and finished all my work just as Mother called 'Cooee – your breakfast's getting cold.'

Mother didn't say anything; I didn't say anything; but we hadn't seen my father all week. We were used to him not coming in at night, but we worried about him nevertheless. Since Dorothy May had gone – his driving mare, the very engine of his life – he had seemed at a loss. He had taken to walking about with a stick. It was this that gave me the clue.

When I was milking that morning I noticed, through a split in the boarding between the cowhouse and the stable beyond, the shiny, white, knuckle-bone top of his stick. I kidded myself that he might be asleep. But as the milk foamed up in the pail my doubts increased.

I was good at putting things out of my mind: last night's unfinished homework, this morning's shortage of milk. I don't think it was fecklessness. It was part of my self-preservation technique. But this was Saturday. It was Whit weekend.

John arrived in time for lunch.

'It was hot on the bus,' he said.

'Let's go to the river,' I said. Poor Mother didn't have time to say 'Wait till your dinner's gone down.'

'I'll see where the Chesneys are,' said John.

'Can I come too?' said Belle. To go with the Chesneys we all thought was fun. I was not in their circle, those bright-eyed, finely balanced, fierce, magnetic Celts. But John was. He had only to send up a smoke-signal, it seemed, and they would appear: Vic, black-haired and blue-eyed; Bob, chestnut and freckled with charm. The jackdaw and the jay.

And, in less time than it takes to tell, they were there outside our house. And their complement of cars had grown to two.

'Squat in the dicky,' Vic said to Belle. 'Peter can ride on the towels on the tank.'

'All right?' said Bob.

'All right,' said Vic.

'It's steaming hot,' said John.

'You'll soon cool off,' said Bob. 'We'll give it stick and make it quick!' He'd been in the RAF.

'Where are we going?' said Vic.

'To the Severn at Montford Bridge,' said Bob.

'Why not the Mill?' shouted Belle, but her voice was drowned in the throttle.

My hair flew off my head; aircraft slowed down; and men in a hayfield leapt up to see what the hell was going by.

Belle put a towel round her head. The buffeting wind nearly tore it away.

'Oh my heart!' she shrilled.

'Never mind your 'eart, Ada – 'ang on to yer 'at!' shouted Vic.

Tears and salt mucus streamed from my eyes and nose. Hedges, ditches, woods and fields flew by. We de-tailed a cock pheasant and scattered the coots by New Pool. It was better than being on a train. Such houses as there were between Nibs Heath and Forton aerodrome, like the Diggorys' with its worn-out thatch, now vanished into thin air. But when we reached the orchards and landscaped gardens of Montford Bridge, its garage, toll house and pub, we slowed to show respect. A little dip along the A5 road and there was the bridge; and there – incredibly far below, it seemed – was the river, broad and deep and irresistible.

'All right?' said Bob.

'All right,' said Vic, who – lanky and lean of limb – dived in with very little splash.

John followed, but stayed under; then came up with unaccustomed difficulty.

'What's the matter?' we shouted from the bank.

'I've got something stuck in my foot.'

'Hold on!' Bob and I armed him up onto the grass.

'It's a rusty old bicycle wheel,' said Belle, and before we could speak she had wrenched a spoke out of John's big toe.

'It's gone clean through,' said Vic, who had now no zest for swimming left.

'The cleaner the better,' said Belle, who was on a pre-nursing course at the Tech.

We soon dried off in the sun. A flick of a towel and a couple of 'All rights', a 'Put your foot down, Bob,' from Vic, 'and make it quick', and we were coolly home again.

It was only after we had milked that afternoon that I told John about the stick. He went quietly by himself to see. It must have been a terrible shock to him to find his father hanging from the stable beam. He made no fuss. My mother knew what we should do. We had to tell the parson first.

'You leave it all to me,' he said: most helpful words at a time like that. I only remember the police activity, the search for a note, the grey blanket covering his body and the old washer-woman coming to help Mother and perform the laying out. How marvellous at such times such lowly people are!

The neighbours who withdrew before, withdrew still further now. We put our trust in God and the parson; and Dad was buried among the family graves in that part of the churchyard which looks out to the morning sun, to lands his father loved for even fewer years than he. His stone is simply engraved with his name; but there is in the village another memorial which records his bravery in the war. It stands outside the house where he was born.

Left is the hard and cold

The rest of that summer I try to forget. The hay, though cut, lay black and rotting in the field. July was wet, but August was wetter still, with nearly six inches of rain. The hens stopped laying and, cold-footed, moped about. The cockerels drooped their tails. The cows stood hump-backed in the field. And Topsy, who opened gates and gave us children wonderful freedom when we were young, grew weary with age and loneliness. She missed my father and Dorothy May. She opened her last gate: to the churchyard.

She lay there stiff and white, an evil-looking discharge running from her back-passage under her still-arched tail.

I called the vet, but I knew it was too late. I knew she had eaten some yew, that plant which is poisonous in every part. Rigor mortis had set in. Tears filled my eyes. To think that she who loved to dance and arch her tail would never bite and open gates again!

'Send for the vet,' had always seemed the saddest words of my childhood. 'Send for the knackerman,' were sadder still.

Eventually we succeeded in getting some hay into our charred shell of a barn – that barn which John and I (aged four and five) had set ablaze one year when the summer – and our pond – were so dry that firemen were hard-pressed to find water to put the fire out. We bought a tarpaulin from F. H. Burgess of Shrewsbury which turned out to have cost more than the hay was worth. We sold some cows, thinking to cut our coat according to our cloth. But nobody knew what a wicked winter lay ahead.

There is one job worse than cutting grass; that's clearing snow. You do it in the first place in the hope that it will help it on its way. It only makes paths slippier.

I don't know when it came, that first white dust of dawn. I only know it stayed. We put straw round the pump. At all cost we must keep that free from frost.

The cows could still drink from the pit by the school. In the corner there stood an oak tree – the one we used to climb at playtime; out of bounds and free, you could hide in that oak from your teacher, from your friends, from your enemies, even from yourself. Looking at it, I could see, as in a book of puzzles, hidden in its branches, the faces of successive children who had scrambled in its boughs. And always at its base, whatever the weather, the water was clear. There I took the cattle to drink. It gave them exercise. They steamed and slurped in the hard bright sun. I cracked the ice along the edge of the pit with an axe. Each day the chunks grew thicker and more untidy on the surface, welded together by frost. Each day the free zone by the oak tree dwindled, till there was only a fragile neck of water, fringed with a lacy ruff of ice. But we persevered, my breathy beasts and I. We glowed, it seemed, with health. My old school mistress – always an apostle of fresh air – came out to congratulate us. We were, she said, a sign of life about the place. There came the day when even she could not get to school and the cows and I performed our drill without an audience.

Funny how uncouth I became with the cows. I forgot my passion for Chopin out there in the exercise yard of my prison world of snow, slopping out. Every day the muck heap rose to steamier, strawier heights above the contours of the past. New Himalayas to be freshly capped with snow each night, or rimed with frost. And all our footprints – dogs', cats', cows' and hens' – all covered over, cancelled out. And urine stains that sizzled for a while in hollows, all hushed up . . . It was a magic, silent, lonesome world. I crept about on six-inch, snow-encrusted soles, like the last survivor in Siberia.

The church bell rang – the old tin can, ting tang – but nobody marked the path across our fields to church. An owl in one of the yew trees would have done as well. The parson said the daily service to himself; and took it out on us on Sunday with a lengthier litany, all Ten Commandments or the Athanasian Creed. ('As also there are not three incomprehensibles, nor three uncreated, but one uncreated and one incomprehensible.') *Hyperion* held no fears, *Endymion* was easy, after that.

Indoors, cocooned in sleep and poetry, we felt secure. There was plenty of coal and wood; plenty of pork from the pig. Hams and flitches that had hung in muslin from hooks in the ceiling for years came down: it was easier now to count the hooks. There were apples in the cellar, potatoes in the hall. It was like Badger's house. There were built-in cupboards everywhere full of forgotten preserves. Larders like dungeons and attics like eyries made our house like a fortress. Even the slates which would slide off the roof in a high wind were sealed in by the frost, and bound by the snow.

Outside, the milk churns stood like cowled snowmen by the gate: Mother called them the White Company. Ginger, our miraculous milkman, came sooner or later, whistling as usual, hair bristling with frost, tyres bristling with chains.

The postman seldom failed to come, even when it meant coming on foot, bringing us news from abroad – which could be almost anywhere – for Mother was a great letter-writer. He hung exhausted on the door and shouted 'Can you hear me, Mother?' as if he bore an SOS.

One day the pump, our lifeline, froze. We set fire to the straw lagging to melt the ice and watched him burn like a guy. Old sacks, like clothes clamped round his body, burned as well. Charred wisps of straw twirled, wriggled and writhed in the air and settled desultorily as airy cinders at his feet. He looked like a naked iron man, whose body we had never properly seen before. We raised his hat from his head to see if he had water on the brain, then shook him by the hand. He coughed and spat and demanded his clothes back. We were only too willing to give him all we had – and a new overcoat of straw for extra warmth.

Water was the source of my strength at the piano – hot water, from the boiler by the fire. I would stoke up after milking at night; go out again – pitch-fork in one hand, hurricane lamp in the other; carry wads of hay from the stack to fodder the cows for the night; sweep up; close all the doors; return to the house; stamp my boots; strip off my working clothes and plunge my arms in piping hot water from the boiler. Then I would take them, red and steaming and sterilize them in the boiler itself. Free and flexible now, I would dry them on a towel which had been warmed by the fire. Then I was ready for the Appassionata, the Polonaise

41

Fantasie, the Revolutionary Study or even the Winter
Wind . . . Unfortunately the temperature in the Empty
Room with no fire soon counteracted all that: I had to
go back to the kitchen to thaw out.

Nobody took any notice of me and my antics. Mother
worked closely with wool, knitting or darning by the
fire, her attention invisibly wired to the radio. My sister
sat, feet screwed under her, and fingers twirling hair,
knitting her brow over *Trilby*, *The Constant Nymph*, *The
Blue Lagoon*. Mother always read in bed, long after she
had finished her work downstairs: Ursula Bloom and
Vicki Baum and *Gone With the Wind* (again). And to
help withstand this siege there were stout volumes of
Pendennis, *The Newcomes* and *Vanity Fair* in the Empty
Room.

Thus we lived, sealed off from the world. Nobody,
or nearly nobody, visited us: certainly not my Priory
friends. (Dickie would not have called it a corner of
Paradise if he had seen our place now.) The only
one who had any knowledge of the harsh reality of
country life in winter was Martin who lived beyond
Baschurch at distant Weston Lullingfields; but he, by
temperament and upbringing, was completely removed
from the rawest aspects of life at Church House. He was
an only child, studious and entirely 'given to books'. He
had read Virginia Woolf and claimed acquaintance with
the Metaphysical Poets. Upright, pale and yellow, he
had a lot in common with Aunt Alice: the same slightly guarded smile, the same preposterous cock-pheasant
laugh. Waspish and whimsical, with an acid eye for the
ironical or absurd, he displayed both self-confidence
and doubt, so that when he was mimicking others he
seemed also to be mocking himself. Some fine Sunday
afternoon, Martin would bowl up on a bike and stay
for tea. But not now, not in mid-winter.

Once a week, of course, the butcher and baker broke
through: steaming, burly relievers of the Siege. Once a

month, perhaps, our grown-up cousin Margery would come to set the ladies' hair and stay the night. While my sister and mother sat like dummies in one room, I would thunder away on the piano in the next. Margery would leave them 'to set', creep in, sit down beside me on the long piano stool and lower her head.

'Play "Jesu Joy of Man's Desiring",' she would say and, as always, her presence made me calm and gave me confidence.

But generally the chords I struck were turbulent; they split the candle-glow. Chords of revolutionariness – the cries of a pent-up soul.

Playing with Fire

Friday, the twenty-eighth of February. The moon, full-face, appeared above the cowhouse door. I looked again. It couldn't be the moon. Not yet.

It was Myfanwy, the dairymaid from the Big House – Myfanwy who smelt of cheese-cloth, milk and dairy steam, whose skin was always slightly moist; a pretty girl with a pretty name and pretty daisy-petal teeth; dumpy, yes, with pink piano legs but a fondness (off duty) for rabbit-fur gloves, tippets, collars and cuffs, honeycomb berets crocheted and cosy, yellow, pink or white, and bootees (with fur) and perfume (Devon violets).

'Just thought I'd come and see if you'd finished.'

'Of course I've finished. Just stripping off.' You could tell Myfanwy anything. It wouldn't go any further. She was plasticine in my hands. You could roll her up, put her away, do what you liked . . .

'You shut the fowl up?'

'No. You going to do them for me?'
'We could do them together – last time. I'm leaving,
you know.'
'Leaving the Big House? When?'
'Tomorrow. It's my last ee-vening. Come to share
it with you.'
My mind went back to a cold, clear, starry night in
the war when I first put my arm round a girl: Phoebe,
who was also as round and warm as a dumpling.
'I feel safe with you,' she told me, as the searchlights
raked the sky over Nibs Heath and Dorniers drifted
back to Germany. There was a new moon then, as there
would be tonight. I was wearing my ATC uniform –
the tunic of which I still wore to do the milking in. I
pointed out the Plough, the Pleiades, Cassiopeia . . .
'What pretty names!' said Phoebe, impressed.
'And Orion – see, like a strong man. Three straight
stars for his belt – and a cluster, a star nursery just below
it.'
She gripped my belt and stars stirred in my loins.
Myfanwy resembled Phoebe. You had the feeling
that she, like her predecessor, did not have to be a
maid. That night she was wearing chinchilla gloves
which I, mistakenly, called coney-fur. Her hat was like
a cushion of sea-pink; her eyes like love-in-a-mist.
'It's nice, that old blue uniform.'
'Didn't bring me any luck. Failed my aircraft recog-
nition test in it – and doesn't help me in telling coney
from chinchilla,' I laughed.
' 'Ello!' We were joined by John the waggoner's
lad who worked at the Big House too.
'What you doin' 'ere, Fanny?'
'What's it look like? Same as you, I should think.
Standing here, aren't I?' Their voices, their faces swam
behind rising clouds of breath and the smoke from
John's cigarette.
'Yo done the eggs?'

'What eggs?'

'The ones fer the egg man. It's Friday night. Yo'd be'er look slippy, 'e'll be 'ere at seven o'clock.'

Reminded of her duty, Myfanwy turned to go.

'They're all clean, anyway,' she called. 'I've only got to put them in the crates.'

'We'll see ya, then,' said John, winking at me. 'A nice bitta 'ole.'

John came inside. We were glad to close the cowhouse door on that east wind.

'Bitter, inna it?' I said to John. Briskly we foddered the cows and bedded them down for the night.

I had had my tea. We slipped round the fowlhouses in our little field, closing up the bob-holes as we went. Then, crossing Church Lane, we looked in on three old mares which were all that John had left over at the Big House farm, stamped our boots on the mat at the servants' door, and scampered up the stairs to his room. Somewhere in the wall was a knot-hole through which, John said, you could see the Lady of the House on a Friday night taking a bath. A corridor linked the three rooms which formed this wing of the house. They were partitioned with wood: long, low-ceilinged rooms with odd angles and beams. The maids' room was the furthest along, of course.

John's bedroom had only one bed, where two or three had been before. On his small chest of drawers was a photo of his dad. His suit hung from a peg on the wall, a poppy in the lapel. Did he ever wear it, I asked. 'No, but I keep the poppy there.' The only other things were a dartboard and a gun. His favourite trick, he said, was to fire the gun off at the dartboard, rush to the knot-hole and see what ripples he had caused in the bath. You could see from the state of the dartboard – and the wall – they were used to John's gun in the house.

You could say that I was a familiar of John's. He had once shown me all round the house.

'See, Er's got twenty-two paira shoes,' he announced, opening his mistress's wardrobe door.

'I can only count twenty-one,' I declared.

'Well, Er's got one on, anna 'er! Where's your common?' he bellowed and shrilled in my ear.

John's employers were often out: Shows (Im and Er), WI (Er), Young Farmers, Old Farmers, NFU (Im), and Whist Drives (Er).

John was, in some ways, privileged. Anyone who has to do with horses or sheep on a farm is privileged: they are exempt from most other duties. But they work hard, awkward hours and, being devoted to their charges, are easily exploited, as John was exploited by Im. But he would not give up the horses; he would not give up his gun.

'I'm up when others is in bed,' said John. 'I cun come an' go as I please.'

Black sheep, satyr, dangerous to know, he moved on the fringes of my mixed-up world. He tickled trout. He robbed girls' nests. ('But not too close to 'ome, mind – you don't tread on your own muck-'eap.') He never lifted an aitch. He was handsome in his well-grown, well-groomed way; always smart in his breeches and leggings and his well-made hacking jacket, with its one vent in the back. Oh, John could run with a horse at Hall, Wateridge and Owen's monthly sale at the Raven Yard in Shrewsbury: 'Clear the way, gentlemen! Let's see 'm trot! That's the style!' I was always excited to be in his company.

'Little bit lonesome, little bit blue, cleanin' my rifle, dreamin' of you,' he sang (or squeaked) as he sat on the bed, lazily drawing the string through the barrel, time after time. His cigarette drew attention to his full lips and half-closed, dreamy eyes.

'Phallic symbolism?'

'Eh?'

We talked of old times when there were more men

47

'living in'; of the fire that blazed in the kitchen then, and how we played with it. And them.

'Remember Pickled Dick an' Fancy 'Arry? God, 'ow we teased 'em,' he said.

'Why Pickled Dick?'

'Cos 'e liked pickle – an' Fancy 'Arry said as 'is dick wus so big it oughta bin pickled!'

'They chased me round that kitchen table one night, I'd been giving them lip. Pickled Dick one way, Fancy Harry the other. Course I couldn't get away. And Fancy Harry picked me up, turned me over and sank his choppers into my backside.'

'An' then they showed ya 'ow they made smoke come outta their eyes!'

' "Watch!" he said. "Watch the smoke come down my nose." '

' 'E wus like a bloody stallion, flarin' 'is nostrils. Ooh! I cudda 'it 'im with a 'ammer!'

' "Watch now," he says, grabbing my wrist and pulling me towards him. "Watch my eyes!" He took a deep drag of his cigarette. I saw his adam's apple slip upwards and his whole throat dilate. I watched his Robert Newton eyes go rolling round and felt the pain under my forearm where the cigarette had stabbed me at the tenderest spot.'

'Yo wus innocent!' scoffed John.

Innocent was not a word I expected to hear from John's practised lips.

What made him so magnetic? His looks? His musical voice? His smell of horse and stable tack compounded with nicotine, aniseed, essence of sweet cottoncake, linseed and flaked maize?

He stood apart, dark and dangerous, letting legends grow round him. Even Gyp admired John and would go rabbiting with him down the Perry Ground, the Bottom Buildings, the Foxholes, and back to the Mound where, sometimes, I would hear the crack of the four-ten and, in the morning, find the tell-tale smudge of a rabbit's head-blood crimsoning the snow. 'Got 'im right between the ears!' He'd click his gun and holler: 'For – 'tis my delight of a shinin' night, in the season of the year!'

That high tenor voice was part of his charm: that and the rakish cap, the prominent adam's apple, the shapely nose, the long fringed lashes on his half-closed eyes . . .

'I wish we 'ad that fire now!' He sat closer to me, bringing his prominent everything else more into view.

'Tractors – them's the things fer the future. Go anyw'eer – even on this snowy ground. No fresh 'osses comin' on. Mares too owd ta breed frum. No proper waggoner's wage. Owd Ince retired. 'E udna do nowt if 'e'adna retired. Pick up one or two rabbits now an' agen. An' all them turmits still in the groun'. They'll be awright, under the snow. Better'n all that beet in a sea uv mud afore Chris'mus – cuddna get it off the fild. Now it's all fruzz. Nothin' wuss than beet that's fruzz.'

I looked round the room. No shelf of books: no *Uncle Tom's Cabin*, no *Huckleberry Finn*. No radio with fretwork front: no Irish Half Hour, no John McCormack, no Monday Night at Eight.

John was still dreamily cleaning his gun. He was passing the weight back and forth, passing the time . . .

'Hisht!' He nudged my knee. There was a swishing and swilling of flushed water swallowed by the lavatory pan; then a hissing of taps turned fully on into the bath.

John started singing again: 'Cleanin' my rifle, dreamin' of you . . . ' Back and forth the shuttle went, the hard-worked string with the weight on one end, the bit of oiled rag on the other, with soothing regularity. Soothing, too, was the singing and gurgling that came from the pipes. The *pipes*! What if John fired his gun and burst a pipe!

He continued in a trance.

I was struck by the fineness of his hands: the big thumb joints, the well-shaped nails. Clean; surprisingly clean. They, the hands of the silent fisherman, could tickle a trout and control a ton-weight horse. They reminded me of my father's. They coaxed the plough-handles; they fondled the gun.

There were other echoes of my father in John: the half-closed, dreamy eyes, the spillage of ash, the laughter and the seriousness.

'What do ya do with yer time?' he asked.

'I lose myself between the covers of a book.'

'I lose myself between the covers of my bed.' He smiled and looked at his watch. Seven o'clock.

'No hotwater bottle?'

'Bloody 'ell, no!'

'Spartan.'

'Eh?'

He picked out a cartridge from a box – red, brass-headed, gleaming and dangerous. I edged away.

' 'S'matter? Ya nervous?'

I felt uncomfortable. What was he going to do?

He dropped the cartridge into the chamber, but did not straighten or cock the gun. He laid it on the bed.

A motor swept into the yard, lights swinging in an arc. Brakes juddered. The engine stopped. A door banged.

'It's only the egg man,' John said.

More splashes next door.

'Er's gotta be at the whist drive by eight.' He checked his watch.

'What about Im?'

' 'E'll be gladuva rest.'

'No dog?'

'No dog at all.'

'I feel like a square peg in a round hole,' I gulped, to try to express the discomfort I felt.

'Eh?' said John, opening his eyes with sudden alarm.

He picked up his gun, straightened it, cocked it, and fired.

'It inna Er,' he whispered at the hole.

'Who is it then?'

'Yo look!'

I pressed my eye to the hole. It was Myfanwy, struggling into her slippers and barely holding on to her towel.

'Two cracked eggs!' called a voice from downstairs.

'That's Er,' said John. Tattoo of footsteps up the stairs.

'Myfanwy!' Rat-a-tat-tat on the bathroom door. 'And why are you taking a bath, may I ask? And what a smell of cheap scent!'

'Devon violets,' I hissed in John's ear.

'Go to your room at once – and stay there until you go home tomorrow!' G-rrunch.

'Er's locked 'er in! But I knows w'eer Er kips the key!' Tattoo of footsteps down the stairs. Indignant cough.

'Er's got the 'uff – like a cow with 'usk!' John's remarks were classics of unspoilt rawness.

He passed his gun to me, picked out a cartridge from the box by the bed, sucked in air through his teeth, and said: 'Well? You goin' to 'av a go?'

'I'd like to,' I said.

'All ya need is the back-up.' He put the cartridge in his pocket, then looked at his watch. 'C'm'on,' he said. 'Downstairs!'

'What's the idea?'

'Yo'll see.'

From the cart shed we saw Im and Er go out. It

51

was a favourite look-out squat: the dropped shafts of a retired muck cart.

'Walkin'? Not drivin',' said John.

'Chaste, the feel of a gun,' I said as we sat there in the moonlight.

'Eh?'

'The wood is as smooth as a maiden's cheek.'

'Yo've got it bad,' said John. He took the gun and laid it in the cart. 'C'm'on,' he said.

I followed him to the stackyard. A white owl, like a small angel of death, flew over to its niche in an oak. It stood with its back to us, swivelled its head and fixed me with one apple-pip eye. Minutest movements and sounds registered with astonishing clarity and ease in the frost-charged air: a quicksilver cat, the last prayers of a mouse, a yowking fox in the wood, querulous mallards – 'dirty drakes', John called them – on the iced-up pool, the hoot of a tawny owl over the Mound, and the assembled shuffles, scuffles, grunts, wheezes and groans – the signals of dominance and despair – from the riff-raff of creation that found refuge in the barn.

Here was sweet-smelling hay for the horses, clovery and fine; and, at the other end, wheat that had not yet been threshed.

The clean-cut haystack, its sheer vertical surfaces and jutting edges sharply etched, its lower platform silvery and inviting, smiled in the moonlight.

'It's like a quarry,' I said. 'A limestone—'

'Ssh! You'll start the guinea fowl.'

I looked up. Ranged on one rafter were some rogue Rhode Island reds: a few repining pullets and a curious, soliloquizing cockerel, blinky-eyed; on another were the ghostly half-wild guinea fowl.

'Better'n a dog about the place at night,' said John. 'They'm use'ta me.'

He picked up a ladder, left upright at one of the high cliffs of hay. I offered to take one end.

'Don't need any 'elp.'

Without knowing anything about fulcrums and levers, he pivoted it perfectly on one shoulder, turned, and
walked back in the direction of the house.

'Er fancies you,' he said.

The moon, her light enhanced by snow, was high
and nearly free of cloud. Frost winked on gates, fences
and leeward surfaces of walls where snow had not built
up. We were figures in an unreal world: John coupled
with his ladder, the shadow of the ladder coupled with
the shadow of John, advancing in silhouette, as if on
stage, performing a duet.

'Me an' my shadder,' I started to sing.

'Hisht!'

He propped the ladder up to Myfanwy's window,
bade me stick my foot on the bottom, and ran up,
skipping rungs, with practised ease.

'C'm'on,' he said.

'Oh, John!' A whispered voice.

'Yo'd be'er wrap up.'

Myfanwy was through the window and halfway
down the ladder before she realized she still had her
slippers on.

'Just a minute, better get my bootees.'

'No knickers!' cracked John, behind his hand to me.
'I'll slip the ladder in the cart shed till later. I'm goin'
fer a drink.'

What did he mean? There was no pub in our
village. It was three miles to the nearest at Nesscliff,
over exhausting tracts of drifted snow. Cider from the
cellar? John had no fear. It was only me who was afraid
of the dark.

'Fanny'll take ya 'ome.'

John was a pagan, worse than Huck Finn.

We didn't go home. We made for the hay: that

53

platform, silvery and smiling, which so invited us. The wind had dropped. We felt each other's warmth.

Presently I felt something else: sticky and wet between my legs.

'More cracked eggs!'

'Who's bothered!'

My hand went straight to the point. Her pubic hair was bristly as cut hay – 'like a pan-scrubber,' I said.

'The bob-hole's open.' She rolled to me.

That night I entered what was for me new territory. 'My soul, there is a country far beyond the stars . . . '

'Go on,' said Myfanwy; 'that's nice.'

'I don't know any more,' I said. I lay back, warm and fulfilled. The first-quarter moon broke through the cloud. Myfanwy leaned over to me and smiled. 'Phoebe,' I sighed: 'bright, radiant moon and sun combined.'

'Phoebe? Who's she?'

Caught out, I covered up.

'Goddess of the moon,' I said.

Love closed on daisy-petal teeth.

'Ssh!'

A shot. A battering of pellets on the sheet-iron roof.

'Stone the crows!'

Panic among the displaced Rhode Islanders and the yakkety guinea fowl overhead: 'Go-back! Go-back! Go-back!'

A fur-covered something, powdered with snow, descended on my face.

'It's my bitta rabbit fur,' Myfanwy yelled. 'He's been in my room! He's seen all I got!'

'Mairzy doats an' dozy doats an' liddle lamsy divey . . . ' John's thin voice squeaked through the blowing of gaskets among the guinea fowl, the consternation of the cock, and the shrieking of the panic-stricken hens.

'How did you get into my room?'

'Same way as you got out.'

'I thought you knew where the key was?'

'Er musta took it with 'er. C'm'on, let's get you back.'

Light snow was falling on the stackyard gate, the owl-frequented oak, the oil-tank by the tractor-house, the warm pigsties where no snow ever lay, and on Myfanwy's lighted window-sill.

He had left the light on of course, and the ladder up.

'I'll need Er to give me a reference,' Myfanwy said, respectfully.

'That was like the whiff of grapeshot with which the young Napoleon made his mark,' I said to John.

The words were whisked away by the stinging wind and the spinning, whirling snow. If the window had been on the other side of the house the wind might have blown the casement off.

'What if I fall?' were Myfanwy's last faintly audible words.

'We'll ketch ya if ya do!'

We left the ladder in the cart shed for the night.

'No 'arm,' said John. I detected a slight odour of beer. There were tyre tracks to the garage door, just filling up with snow.

'You found the key you wanted, then?'

'Of course.'

It was snowing heavily as I left the scene.

'It'll cover our tracks,' I said, 'masking the day's misdeeds and leaving the world all set for a clean start tomorrow.'

'Eh?' said John.

Sardines and Murder

There was Murder at the old malthouse in March. Such revels we had never known before. There were stories of my father's large family and circle of friends chasing the maids through rambling farmhouses and letting their hair down in the past; but this was the first real party we had had. Presents for birthdays, yes; but parties, no. Laura and I were eighteen. Whatever happened tonight, we had already lived it in our dreams.

The fire in the Empty Room roared like a furnace. The milking still had to be done. The girls had to do extra dusting, cleaning the house from top to bottom. Mother did the cooking, but we all promised to help with the washing up – in daylight – tomorrow. Coal had to be got in, oil-lamps checked.

'Better make sure the cellar's not flooded! And tidy up the attics, if you're going to play all over the house!' Mother was scrupulous about holes and corners. 'And I've just run my finger over the piano lid. Take a duster to it now' – this, to me. 'Well, you use it!'

We only had the one tin bath. It looked as if the piano was going to be cleaner than the pianist.

Tea was a snack and a torment. The sight of all those sandwiches, cakes, trifles and fruit-salads in the kitchen and my sisters smugly guarding them made me feel like an outsider, which I was.

'You fill up with toast and dripping,' they said. 'There's no butter left.'

I took the hurricane lamp and, in the familiar ring of light thrown round the byre, I started pinging the bottom of the pail. Thinking of who might be coming to the party, I was soon warmed by the milk, the cows' breath and the sweetness of the freshly laid-out hay.

There would surely be Dickie who was sweet on Belle. There would surely be Sergeant Latto of the Army Cadet Force with the 'amorous eyes'. He had sat with his arm round Barbara at her party in broad daylight. Barbara who had long, black, curly hair, Merle Oberon eyes, small features, an alabaster skin, and didn't look a bit like a country girl. She was the daughter of an agricultural engineering contractor. Agricultural engineering contractors' daughters did not have to soil their hands.

'Oh, hello Barbara!' I was practising my introduction. Hand-milking – the cow looking on indulgently – is good for practising this sort of thing. 'I saw you in town on Saturday.'

'I wasn't in town on Saturday!' said Penny Bowles. Peep-bo, as we called her, was a girl who had come to Little Ness as an evacuee and limpet-like had chosen to stay. She was grinning at me from the cowhouse door. The bucket slipped between my legs but fortunately stayed upright.

'I'm early,' the teeth announced. Red lipstick framed the blank remark.

'I was learning my lines,' I said defeatedly.

'Have you got many more to do?'

'What, lines?'

'No, cows.'

'Oh, three more, I think. Would you like to go in?'

'I'm in.'

'I mean in the house.'

'Oh, I'm warm enough.' She rubbed her arms and gave herself a hug. She was as tall as a lamp-post. Her face shone like the light on top. You had to give Peep-bo full marks for gas if not for electricity. And for persistence . . .

Just as I was reckoning ten minutes for the next heifer and five minutes for the two 'dry' ones at the end, I noticed the in-calf Ayrshire lying down. She was in a stall by herself, lying tight-bagged with her hind legs fairly wide-stretched out. She was slack around the tail.

'She's going to calve,' I sighed.

'Oh, jolly good!'

'Jolly bad!' I said. 'She may be hours. She's very big. There might be twins. I'll be popping out and in all night.'

'Oh, I'll pop with you!'

'It's not a pretty sight.'

'Oh I'm not queasy.' *Queasy.* Was there ever a word more calculated to expose the Peep-bo's prominent teeth?

I parked Penny with Mother in the kitchen and wondered where the hell I was going to strip down and wash.

Cousin Margery had come from Baschurch with her curling tongs and had wrought a transformation on our girls. I had never seen them in lipstick before; and there they were being tweaked on top with irons first laid on an evil-smelling spirit-lamp, then dexterously twirled in the air, and finally squeezed into pieces of hair held up by a comb. Methylated magic! Their faces glowed in a blue haze while the yellow flame leaped and waved about.

'Keep it well away from the food,' my mother said.

Margery had savoir-faire. She made you feel the party would be a success, just by being there. Your self-esteem went up a notch. If there was a young lady more beautiful than Margery, we had not seen her. If there was a voice more reassuring, we had not heard it. Margery had class. All would be well.

But there was the Ayrshire to think about. And where was I going to wash?

'Nobody will see you behind the screen,' said my mother, matter-of-fact.

'Not if they don't look,' I muttered.

'Everybody's looking at us,' said Belle.

'Who's everybody?' said Penny.

'You,' said Laura, cockily.

I was glad she felt that way. It was *our* birthday and she was home from the Land Army. We all made a fuss of her; and she looked lovely in her little red dress and make-up to match.

'Some day my Prince will come . . . ' I whistled as I splashed behind the screen. She had always been the Cinderella – and Margery our Fairy Godmother.

'That's the front door!'

'They're here!'

'It's seven o'clock!'

'Don't panic,' said Penny. 'I'll ush them in.'

'Sit them down in the Empty Room,' said Mother. 'See if the fire's all right.'

'Phew!' I threw a towel round my loins and paddled up the back stairs with a candle to light me to the old play-room where, Mother said, she had laid out all my clothes: vest, socks, shirt, my Hepworth's suit. We were still wrestling with detached collars in those days, studs back and front.

'I've got no stud!'

'I have,' called Margery, miraculously. 'I got two in town today; they're in my handbag. Here.' She handed them to me on the stairs. 'I got them for Daddy, as spares.'

'Saved again! Thanks a lot.'

'My, you look smart!'

'Yes, and I've got all my old clothes ready for when the Ayrshire starts to calve.'

Everybody came who should have come; and one or two who shouldn't. Dickie, Martin, Latto; Barbara, Penny, Joan and Eileen; 'Jeece' (C. C.), 'Piff' (P. F.) and 'Alphabet' (A. E. J. T.) – all Davieses, but no relation. Even Kite came. Late. His wheel had slipped.

'What shall we play then? Sardines?'

'How do you play Sardines?'

'Well, someone has to go and hide and then we all go round in the dark trying to squeeze in with them – without making a sound. If they hide in a cupboard or a wardrobe it can get quite interesting.'

It was. Our house was all cellars and attics and there was no problem about darkness. There was an oil-lamp in each of the three main rooms and the rest of the house was free-range Erebus.

Dickie was appointed hider and in no time had a closet full of giggling girls and was still trying to get more in. Others had formed a splinter group with Latto under a bed. I slipped out to see what the Ayrshire was doing. Two white-tipped feet, like sticks of rhubarb pointed out.

I rushed back to change into my old things. Barbara was helping Mother in the kitchen.

'Can I come?' she asked, incredibly.

'Yes, if you don't mind missing your supper,' I said.

'I don't eat,' she said.

'What an economical wife you'd make,' I cracked.

'I'd cost you a lot in clothes,' she responded, trumping my ace.

The head was out and with a short pull the whole

calf came sloppily out onto fresh, clean straw. I parted the membrane from the muzzle, put my fingers in
his mouth and drew him within reach of his mother's
searching tongue. I parted his legs. I knew it.

'A bull! Now why couldn't you have given me a
heifer?'

'I'm sorry?' said Barbara.

'I don't mean you. I wanted a heifer to breed from.'

'Will he have to die?'

'Not this one,' I was glad to be able to say. 'He's
very well bred; by an AI bull.'

'What's that?'

'Artificial insemination.'

'Never mind,' she said, 'he wasn't artificially deliv-
ered.' She was quick, this porcelain, potential farmer's
wife. 'Do you know,' she said, 'I live on a farm, but I've
never seen a new-born calf. We only keep tractors . . . '

We soon had the calf on his wobbly feet and after
three or four blind shunts in the wrong direction he
was at the teat and foaming with delight.

'He mustn't have too much. We'll come back in an
hour.'

'Oh, can't he stay all night?'

'No, he'll have to go in the calf-kit.'

'Rotter,' she said and pecked me on the cheek.

'What shall we play then?' Supper for the masses
was over and the cupboards were beginning to bulge
again. I stood with a plate of sandwiches in a heavily
disinfected hand.

'Murder.'

'How d'you play it?'

'Well,' said Belle, who had all these things worked
out, 'in this hat are a lot of blank pieces of paper, but
one of them is marked with an X. We all take a pick.
The one who gets the X is the murderer. Ssh! When
the light goes out we all fumble around.'

'Fumble?' said Martin, dyspeptically.

'Well, you know what I mean . . . Now the murderer must keep his X a secret. When the light goes out, he has to touch somebody on the shoulder. He, screaming, drops down dead – the murderer on top of him. Then the murderer runs away. The light goes up and we have to try and guess who did it, see?'

'Can we go all over the house?'

'Yes, if you scream loud enough.'

'Peter can't be the murderer,' said Barbara. 'The victim would smell him.' I could have strangled her.

I don't really know what happened that night. I kept dashing out to the Ayrshire cow who had got down in her stall and did not seem to be able to get up. She had, I was afraid, developed milk-fever. I'd have to call the vet from the kiosk the other end of the village. It was late, but I knew he would come – he always did.

When I had to ring for the vet, I thought of only two things: 'O Happy Band of Pilgrims', which was the number in the hymn book, 224; and 'remember to press Button A'.

The number was obtainable at the kiosk through the post office, just up the road. Frequently in the old days, Mrs Garry had had to shout to a stranded, puzzled, trembling boy: 'Have you pressed Button A?' Whereupon all was made clear. Mr Sinclair's crisp, efficient Scottish tones would come through: 'I'll be there rright away.'

Tonight I remembered to press Button A.

'Mr Sinclair?'

'Speaking.' He was in. Sometimes, he was out on his rounds and his wife answered, always indicating there would be some delay. 'I'll tell him as soon as he returns . . . '

'I'll be there rright away!' His words were some comfort to me for the interruption of my party.

As I stumbled back from the phone-box I could hear the mêlée of voices raised in the dark, signalling the departure of some, if not all, of our guests. I wondered vaguely who was going home with whom.

'Goodnight,' I said to two anonymous bicycles by the gate.

An engine started up, headlamps came on, and a little white hand waved from the agricultural contractor's van which was drawn up by the kerb. The window wound down.

'Goodnight,' came the voice from inside; 'and thanks for the birthday treat. I hope the cow and calf will be all right.'

'Thanks, Barbara,' I called through the smoke of the exhaust.

After that the vet came quickly, injected the cow with calcium in the neck and departed almost in one movement saying, 'She'll be OK in the morrnin'.' He was brisk and adroit and wasted no words.

'And the calf?'

'Och, he'll be all right. Give me a rring if he's not.' My thanks were drowned in three quick revs and a *rhummm!* through the gate.

I checked the top door of the shippon and crossed the cobbles in the frost-clean air. It wouldn't be possible to turn the cows out till mid-April; but would the hay last out till then? An old hen who always roosted in the pear tree by the back door turned, wheezed and winked in the light of my lantern; and Gyp who was, I suppose, her unwitting protector drew a grumble from his chain. Even in old age, in the depths of winter, he always slept in his kennel by the house.

The light was still on in the kitchen and a little flame licked up the empty grate. Face to face at either end of the screen, like two poised effigies in church, sat

63

Kite and Laura, their heads and hands drooped on their raised up knees.

'Ssh! Kite's gone.'

'I thought he had.'

'He's drunk, I think.'

'I'll say he is – he smells worse than the vet.'

'He said his wheel had slipped. He's left his bike by the corn-bin.'

'That's all right, but what else was he doing round the corn-bin?'

'He's been round the back of the furnace-hole . . . '

We knew what was in each other's mind.

'Where the bottles are?'

'I didn't know there was any whisky there. It *is* whisky. It's sweet and sickly.'

Kite had black smudges of old furnace-hole soot on his eyebrow and cheek; and round his collar, where his skin usually glowed butter-bright as when you hold a buttercup under someone's chin to see if they like butter, he'd run his sooty hand. His face was white, his eyelids greeny-grey. Black cobwebs hung about his coat; and one, like tiny beads of rust, ran down his ear.

'He's been telling me all about himself,' said Laura. 'And all about us. He's psychic.'

'He's blotto. Come on, we'll put him on the sofa in the other room.'

'Better leave a note at the bottom of the stairs to warn the others in the morning.'

'And take his jacket off.'

'And loosen his tie.'

'I'll clean his jacket up.'

'He can have my eiderdown.'

We lifted him like a sack of malting barley into the sitting room and dropped him on the sofa. He looked like Endymion in the moonlight.

'Whatever you say, he's very nice.'

'I don't say anything. I just wonder how he found

whisky where I thought there was only sweaty old beer. What did he tell you?'

'He told me that he'd heard so much about this place but never been allowed to come. Now, I think, he doesn't want to go back home.'

'Was he difficult?'

'No. Charming. I've never been spoken to by anybody so polite. But there was a sadness in those blue-grey eyes.'

'Before they shut. We'd better go to bed. Prince Charming can sort his shoes out in the morning.'

Mother was not in the least surprised, next day, to find another mouth to feed.

'You may not be hungry, Kite, but you're having a boiled egg. We won't have fried stuff this morning – I'll spare you that.'

'Thanks,' said the sheepish Kite.

'But you must phone your parents to let them know where you are. They'll be worried sick. A more-disturbing-thing-than-knowing-the-worst-is . . . ' Her voice trailed off in a cloud of steam as she scalded the tea.

'Not knowing the worst,' said I, knowing my mum.

'I put that bottle there years ago,' she said, with a twinkle in one half-closed eye. 'About a quarter full.'

'Three quarters empty.'

'Well, more empty than full. As you may guess, when your father had finished with it.'

'I bet it's more or less empty now.'

'More than less,' said Kite.

I took him to the phone-box and dialled SHR (for Shrewsbury) 593.

'The Crown Inn,' came the snapped response.

'Kite stayed the night. His wheel slipped.'

'I'll slip his wheel for him—'

'It's all right, Dad.' Kite grabbed the phone. 'I'll be back to do the cellar out.' It sounded like 'the shit house, too,' from the voice at the other end.

'He's in a bad skin.'

'He's always in a bad skin.'

'You don't know what a pleasure it is to be here,' Kite said as I mucked out the cows. 'To me it's like a tonic.'

'You should come more often.'

'I wouldn't be allowed. We're like prisoners at home.'

'Prisoners behind bars?'

'Prisoners behind bars . . . '

I turned my peaked cap back to front on my head and carried in fresh hay. Kite said I looked like those coracle men he'd seen by the river, carrying their upturned vessels on their heads.

I cut fresh wads out with the hay-knife. It flashed like a falchion in the sun. The dwindling stack sank like a sprung mattress under our feet.

'Let me have a go,' Kite asked.

'No,' I said. 'It's one thing to have you laid out with a bottle. It's quite another to be laid out with a knife.'

'The bowie knife!' Kite leapt with unaccustomed verve. The last unbalanced tower-block rocked and I swung into space, leaving the hay-knife scything through thin air. It scattered a few hysterical hens and landed harmlessly beside a stretched-out pig. Pigs do not scuttle straight away. But when they scuttle . . .

We sat down in the smokey-bottomed hay which was mouldy and moist, bleached by sun and blackened by rain.

'Smells like old boots,' said Kite.

And then I told him about Grandad and the hay-knife. Not my grandad, my cousin's – but the only one I ever

66

knew. My cousin Lily had told me the story; her every word was graven on my mind.

It was a dull day, about mid-morning, this time of the year, the same left-over shapes of hay . . . Everything seemed to be under control: the milking done, pigs and poultry fed, breakfast over and the younger children off to school, leaving Lily and her mother and Grandad at home. Her mother was across the field tending a new batch of baby chicks and she (Lily) was scrubbing the dairy utensils. Above the rattle of the buckets she heard Grandad shouting 'Help!' Not knowing where he was, she listened and the repeated calls directed her to the stackyard. She raced through the cowshed, not stopping to close doors, and as soon as she opened the door into the stackyard, there was Grandad looking ashen, holding his arm, the blood spurting up like a fountain all over the door he had not been able to open.

Lily helped him to the house, at the same time screaming for her mother to come quickly. Together they applied a tourniquet. They had no car, so Lily ran to the neighbours across the road and a long way up a field. The neighbour dropped her cheese-making, and drove them to Shrewsbury – straight through the traffic-lights by the station, up Castle Street and a quick turn left, to the Infirmary. Their arrival had nurses and doctors scurrying as Grandad's strength was rapidly waning through loss of so much blood. Without wasting any time they gave him a blood transfusion and an injection of glucose to help counteract the shock. Lily was told that his condition was grave and next of kin should be informed.

During the afternoon, when his condition became more stable, he was taken to the theatre, where a West Indian doctor performed the surgery, reattached the arteries and ligaments and sutured the gash. His condition remained grave and some of the family stayed with him throughout the night. He survived, but lost the use of his forefinger and thumb.

'But how did he do it?' asked Kite.

'Exactly as you might have done,' I said, not realizing I had rattled on almost as fast as Lily had run up that field. 'He was going up the ladder to cut a wad of hay, his foot slipped and he dropped the knife which landed blade-up where he fell with his forearm right across the blade, severing everything to the bone.'

Kite looked white.

'We must see to your bike. But come again, won't you?' I said. He surprised me with a paternal pat on my knee.

'It's the Weights and Measures for me after Easter; a safe and steady job.'

We fixed his bike – a simple thing to do. And Kite rode off, as serious and sober as a judge.

On the Idle Hill of Summer

When green buds hang on the elm like dust
And sprinkle the lime like rain,
Forth I wander, forth I must,
And drink of life again.

'You're mooning about,' my mother said. She was
right. But what else was there to do? What else was
there ever here to do?

As kids we wandered round the Cliffe, the coppy,
the pit, the Mound – our happy hunting grounds – in
company, not always of the best. Now, the only one
of the litter left at home, I was 'a fish out of water, too
much on my own, my head full of Romantic poetry',
my mother said.

I was orbiting the kitchen table, this particular morning in May: May the seventh, the anniversary of the
day we left Wigmarsh and came to Little Ness. My
brother and I, aged five and three. And every year
since, whether we spoke of it or not, we remembered
the day as a landmark in our lives. On the seventh of
May we breathed a fuller, freer air.

I sniffed. 'Smells good!' Mother was doing an extra
mid-week bake. She was making both a rhubarb and a
rabbit pie.

'Aunt Alice is coming – it's her birthday next week.'
'Again?'

Mother first prepared the rhubarb pie, rolling out the pastry for the bottom of the pie-dish like a blanket for the bottom of a bed. Her wedding ring clicked on the rolling-pin. With the deft artistry she brought to all her humdrum tasks, she swung the blanket in; then, taking a knife, she trimmed the surplus edges off. I picked one up and swallowed it with the same sense of triumph that I had felt when I was too small to see over the table and ran the risk of having my roving knuckles rapped.

Now it was Mother who seemed diminutive. Head down and shoulders hunched, she skinned the pink and white sticks of young rhubarb with the knife, leaving curls of inedible string to one side. There was something touchingly innocent about what was left. Cut into cubes and sugared in the dish, it was too tempting for words.

'Get!' was all my mother said, threatening me with the knife.

Next it was the half-grown rabbit's turn. Shining, silvery pink, it acted as a reflector to the dancing flames from the fire. With lightning strokes, my mother worked at its pliant and – to my eye – suppliant form, quartering it, and setting the tiny forelegs, the finely arched rib-cage, the small of the back and the hindlegs into the rabbit-pie dish.

'There are no laughs in Keats,' she said. 'Lord Byron had stolen them all.'

I orbited again.

An inverted egg-cup stood ready to go in the centre of each dish; shaped, one like a hen, the other like a cockerel, they had come originally with Easter eggs, and had played for as long as I could remember a supporting role in the architecture of any rabbit or rhubarb pie.

My mother rolled a second lump of pastry out, from time to time dusting the rolling-pin with fresh flour and all the time reading my thoughts and jutting out an elbow just as I moved too near.

'Each time might be the last . . . '

'For Aunt Alice, you mean?'

She had left four strips of edging from the earlier mixture to one side, but I was not to be tempted again; I knew that they would form the crown, the little knob on the top of each pie which, when baked, would blossom as a newly opening rose.

She was so practical, my mother. She was not to be caught 'wandering between two worlds, the one dead, the other powerless to be born'.

She swung the coverlets on top. They fitted amply, overlapping only as snow overlaps a barrel or a lawn. She did not have to trim. She twirled two of the spare pieces together in the shape of a rosebud and set it in the centre of each pie, thumbed round the border and placed it in the oven by the fire.

'I shall damp the fire down later, then let the rabbit-pie cook slowly, and we'll have it for tea. Now, you go off on your bike!' She brushed her cheek with a floury hand, leaving a comic smudge on her nose. A small veil of hair fell over her face. She sat down. She wanted to be alone.

I had only a reach-me-down bike. I called it the Red Devil. It had dropped handlebars, cable brakes (only one of which, the front, worked), one and a half mudguards, a seat like an albatross's bill, a dodgy cotterpin, a general lack of alignment and no bell – but it did have three gears.

'Behold, I am fearfully and wonderfully made!' I crowed, clicking out of normal into top. My voice, like my vehicle, was cracked. I exulted in my new-found summer strength: the embodiment of swank. For who, aged eighteen with the wind in his open shirt, does not

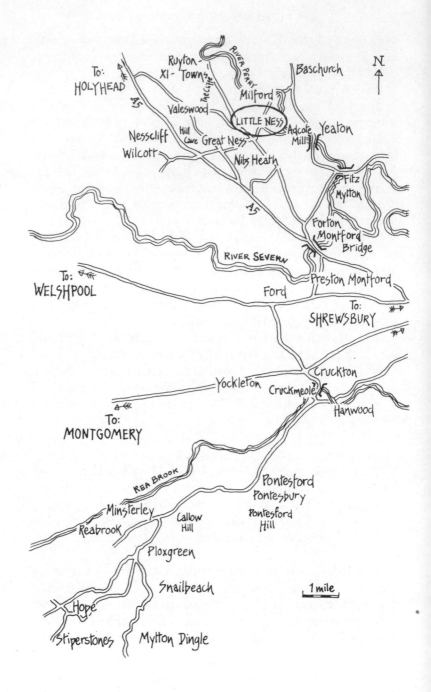

think he is master of the open road. I had a spindly frame, but plenty of strength in my legs. I stood up off the seat and, rocking vigorously from side to side, accelerated down the Great Ness road. Cradled in the crevice of my chest was one dark, curly hair.

'Velocipede!' I yelled, starting a stampede of bullocks in the Poplars Field. I settled on an easy equilibrium, sweeping up hills, swooping down. Via the Ruddiferns, the flat-land elms, the sleek barley fields of Preston Montford, I came to Ford – a route I had often taken on Topsy to see my cousins at Heath Farm. I would not go there today. Past Park Gates and Pavement Gates, I took the turn to Yockleton. 'Dante', my brother's old school friend, had come from there. He read *La Divina Commedia* sitting on his uncle's henhouse floor. I crossed the Montgomery road and stopped on the wooden bridge at Cruckton where the Rea Brook snuffled and guzzled in its trough below the posts and rails and floodwater gauge still clouded with mud and garlanded with weed. The road on this very hot day was powdery dry. We had not seen a dusty road for months.

Bearing right at Cruckmeole, I came to Hanwood, the Shrewsbury–Aberystwyth railway line and larch-fringed Pontesford Hill.

I stopped in the village of Pontesbury, with its forbidding, four-square church, the clock on the tower striking one and children at play in the school yard opposite. The traditional buildings of the school were set up high above the road; the sloping playground, rather cramped, was walled and railed around. A ball bounced into the road by my feet and ran off down the street. A girl appeared, her pretty face with wide beseeching eyes framed between two iron rails. The noise of a heavy roadstone lorry drowned her words. She had shining auburn hair, dark chestnut eyes, and what my sisters called a Cupid's bow. She might have been fourteen. More vehicles roared past, but I retrieved her ball. She smiled and skipped away to tell her friends.

On the opposite side of the road, where the ball had rolled, the post office door stood open to the sun. A range of plain black and white picture postcards was displayed just inside. I picked out one of a long, low cottage in a field: The Nills. It was plain indeed.

'That's where Mary Webb lived,' said the post mistress. 'She used to come in sometimes on her way to Shrewsbury with her flowers to sell in the market.'

'I've just been reading *The Golden Arrow*,' I said.

'Well, that's where she wrote it,' said the lady at the counter. She had blue, attentive eyes, a woolly hat, and a wide, warm smile. I bought the card and a couple of Mars bars and set off in search of Mary Webb, or the golden arrow – 'the wand of willow in the secret cwm'.

Pontesbury was a large village with many shops: almost a town. But it was flanked by hills; strange, familiar hills. It took some working out, but these were the hills I had known all my life – or rather, had not known. I had only seen them from the bedroom windows of our house. Crested or crowned with larch, one was like a mangy old lion asleep, another like a giant staddlestone; and, going on for ever were the long-tailed Stiperstones. It was there, the lady in the post office said, that I should go.

I had never heard or seen so many cuckoos before: they *wantoned* round the hill. There was a huge police station. Could there, I wondered, be so many malefactors in one place? There were chapels: sinners too?

I passed the creamery at Minsterley: Wathes, Cattell & Guerdon. The smell of a creamery takes your breath away. I needed a drink. A shop offered Corona: dandelion and burdock. Try anything once. It swilled down into my stomach and swam back up into my eyes. There was a fireball in the chimney of my nose. Opposite, through tearful eyes, I spotted another gloomy church, another war memorial telling its tale of woe. 'In Glorious Hope . . . '

Hope! That was the road I needed to take. I doubled back across the bridge, sighting again the Rea Brook, another chapel, another inn. Here houses passed for halls; half-timbered and aloof, they had tradesmen's entrances and monkey puzzle trees. What did I know about Hope? A little boy, evacuated to a farm there, had been starved to death.

I was oppressed by another corrugated-iron village hall with auctioneer's notices declaring farms for sale:

DESIRABLE LAND, STOCK, IMPLEMENTS
BY ORDER OF . . .

I was cheered by pretty painted cottages with riverside gardens drenched in sunlit willows overhanging slumbering ducks and wild-eyed polyanthus flowers. Brooks and rivers, I noticed, foster ingenuity in the people who live by them. The smaller the property, the more they trick it out with adornments of a simple, playful kind: chiefly toy windmills, of course. Mayflowers filled the meadows; periwinkle smiled as I passed by, and cow parsley raised a million parasols.

It was hot.

At Plox Green I met the number 18 Midland Red bus, the same that brought the Minsterley and Pontesbury boys to school at the Priory. They were a byword for bad behaviour. Be not deceived by windmills, I huffed, as I tackled the steep climb up to Snailbeach.

The windpump in the field on my left, the small oaks – their heads 'sunning over' with tight-curled, tawny leaves – the wayside stitchwort, the small, tidy farmsteads of the lower hill, so neatly walled and fenced, their hedges newly layed, did nothing to prepare me for the sudden transports – the gasps and breathless gulps, the gradients, the views – that delight the eye and take

75

the legs from under you when you innocently attempt a two-wheeled passage to Snailbeach. The bends! The staggers!

And on one of those bends was perched a shop, blandishing OVUM for laying hens, Virol for nursing mothers, Craven A – more friendly for your throat – and Corona. I was not to be tempted again.

'Difficulties nerve the spirit of a man,' I had read that morning in a letter by Keats.

I passed a little man bearing a big basket on one arm and hopping along like a bird. I, eighteen and nearly six feet tall, ought to be able to get up this hill on a bike.

I came shaking to a halt by a cottage just past the church.

'You want a drink?' asked a couple at their garden gate. They spoke in unison.

'Thank you very much,' I gasped, 'I had no idea!'

'No one ever does,' said the pale-eyed little man in waistcoat and straw hat. 'Come in.'

I dropped my bike and followed them into the house. You weren't generally invited into cottages. There must be something special about this couple, I thought.

'The sun's putting my fire out,' the lady said. 'Sit down.'

The interior of the cottage reminded me of the Thongers' at Nesscliff and the Roberts' under the Cliffe. You could not have got more objects into one room: a chest, a clock, a corner cupboard, a gun on one beam, a ham hanging from another, a harmonium (Mason and Hamlin, Chicago, USA), a weather-glass, a copper kettle, a bobble-fringed mantel lined with pots and ornaments, a table and tablecloth (plush and bobble-fringed) with central vase of flowers, chairs of course – and a settle on which I sat. A lick of flame was palely loitering in the grate.

Such rooms are usually cool and their windows too

small for them to be anything but dim. But they are snug. They smell of food and homeliness.

'Here, this will do you good,' said the little old lady, offering me a glass of water. 'It's from the spring.'

She smoothed her work-worn hands on her pretty print overall, then straightened her hair which was screwed up into a bun on the top of her head. She had quick, bright eyes that gleamed like blackberries. Her husband had removed his hat, revealing a bristly head of grisled hair. Neither seemed disposed to sit, but stood respectfully examining me, smiling and very still, like figures in a frieze.

A brindled cat appeared and, high-tailed, wound its sinuous body round my legs.

'I am honoured,' I remarked.

'Another glass?' the old man asked.

'No thank you,' I smiled. It was very refreshing.

'The grandchildren come for the Sunday School Anniversary the first Sunday in May,' said the lady. 'There's nothing they like better than going with me for a pail of water from the spring just up the road.'

'Is this your church?'

'No. We're Methodists really. We worship at the Baptist chapel at Lord's Hill. Dad's a local preacher, you see. Aren't you, Dad?'

His face shone with a kindly, inner light. A white silk scarf was loosely knotted round his neck. He was, like his lady, as clean as a pin. They had small, particular mouths and well-kept teeth which seemed to add discretion to their speech.

'Father worked in the mine for forty years,' she said. 'He's retired now, of course. Does a bit of gardening, like.'

'Just put my runner beans in, now the elm leaf's like a mouse's ear. I like to see them twice in May.'

'My father used to say that,' I smiled. 'The earth's a bit more thinly spread round here, though,' I added,

77

trying to impress him with my powers of observation.
'It isn't what you h-have, but what you do with what you h-have,' he pointed out. He seemed to have difficulty drawing breath. 'I'm going to prepare myself,' he said to his wife and withdrew to an inner room. His wife went with him solicitously, but, quietly closing the door, returned to talk to me. She patted her chest.

'It's the mid-week meeting at Lord's Hill this afternoon. His breathing's none too good – but the Lord gives the word.' She smiled, still standing. 'It's what keeps him going,' she said.

She told me that they had lost five children. I did not ask how.

A child's sampler on the wall said GOD IS LOVE. Open on the harmonium was 'Though Your Sins Are Scarlet They Shall Be White As Snow'. (Redemption Hymns: I knew that from Aunt Alice.)

I thought of all the men who, since Roman times, had worked in these hills, grimly twisting and turning, humping and heaving, shunting and shovelling, picking and stealing a living from this earth.

A knock on the door, and a shrill voice announced: 'Your tuthree ounces uv sugar an' tay, Missus!'

'Oh, thank you, Knucky,' the lady sang, and I got up to go. 'That's Knucky the carter, that was,' as if referring to a departed spirit. 'Wartime mistletoe, and all!'

'I'll see you down the garden path,' she said. 'Make sure you close the gate.' She smiled. 'There's Knucky disappearing up the road! He used to have a pram, but the wheel dropped off.' I wondered if she was pulling my leg. 'You'll see what I mean if you overtake him – which I doubt.'

She sprinkled the air with these remarks which, coming from one so outwardly staid, seemed almost mischievous.

'There's Mytton Dindle,' she said, pointing into

78

the sun. 'Mad Jack Mytton, the old Shropshire squire,
drove a carriage and pair down that hill for a wager.'

Places up there looked scarred. Communities wore
a haunted aspect, grafted, as they were, to the steep
hillside. What a place for a play!

'Danger round every corner,' I said.

'Yes, mind the cow-pats!'

I had picked up my bike and was standing in a
line of diminishing pie-crusts on the road ahead.

'They're firm,' I said, examining my thin-soled shoes.

'But why Lord's Hill?' I asked.

'Lord Tankerville,' she said. 'He was sympathetic to
the nonconformist miners' wishes and granted them the
land for a place of worship, you see.' She smiled, as if
she had imparted only half a secret. 'Lord Bath owned
all the rest.'

'I see,' I said. Emboldened by this confidence, I
nearly risked a reference to *The Golden Arrow*, that
passage which goes, 'Above the door, with a nervous
and pardonable shuffling of responsibility (apparently
by the architect) were the words, "This is the Lord's
doing".'

'No Abel Woodus plucking his harp?' I mischievously enquired.

'All choirs and brass bands here,' she said. 'We sang
for lead and whistled for coal. Every cottage had its
harmonium, tin whistle and jew's harp. It was music
that kept the flock together, you see. Still does. The
men favoured the brass band, of course. If you could
blow, they used to say, it was enough.' She dimpled
a little and patted her overall again. ' "Yo carry on,
Conductor," one old character used to say – he regularly
arrived late – "I'll catch you up!" '

She smiled again. Another story coming up, I
thought.

Then she told me how, as a little girl, she had gone
to Waller's Brook and found under the bridge, below a

little waterfall, a frying pan with a fish in it. She took it home to her mother for breakfast. It was Christmas Day.

'And of course we grubbed out pignuts in the lane on days like this, and ate "bread and cheese" you know, and sweet briar. But it was not all pignuts and bread and cheese.'

Her mother remembered the opening of the school in 1871 and how, in that first year, every child died bar one – and he was a deaf mute.

'What did they die of?' I asked.

'Scarlet fever,' she said.

Still patting her overall, she told me how on the sixth of March 1891 four local preachers and three Sunday School teachers died when a steel rope broke and the eight-foot cage they were in was reduced to two feet by the impact. A miner's watch ticked on . . . 'We put something in each of the seven coffins,' she said.

I did not ask what.

'The community closed ranks,' she added. And I could see them, like the bereaved fisherfolk of Paimpol in *Pêcheur d'Islande* (my favourite novel) consoling one another and easing their heartache with song. She told me she worked part-time at the school. 'You'll see it if you carry on up.'

'And the chapel?'

'To your left. And if you get tired, under every ruck of rushes there's a spring.' She sent me smiling on my way.

The lane was fringed with ferns and sprigged with broom, rowan and damson trees. The fields smelt of grass and cows. Even the cowflop was sweet.

To Lord's Hill, a little signpost said. I'll go there on my way back, I thought.

A narrow-gauge railway line idled its way between startlingly white spoilheaps of lime-spar or barytes, a by-product of the lead mines which, I knew, was used in the making of paint.

Cottages displayed rustic arches and pergolas, painted waggon-wheels, tubs, bird-tables and timeless topiary. Most, it seemed, had a pigeon loft and a pigsty at the rear.

Buzzards wheeled round the hilltop in the clear blue dome of the sky. The sun bore pitilessly down on me. I saw few small birds: sparrows of course, a yellowhammer, a ticking wheatear, and what might have been a whinchat which flew up from a stump of gorse.

I passed the school. No ball rolled onto the road here. The wall, surmounted by what looked like an eight-foot wire fence, would have kept a bull within bounds. More royal carpet of cowflop, more tin and asbestos homes, nimble, quick-witted sheep (one with a yoke round its neck), stones littered about, an iron bedstead stopping the gap which the handicapped sheep had pushed aside, a female sparrow hawk.

Barbed wire and brambles had snagged the fleeces of half-naked ewes; only their bouncy, half-grown lambs were still intact. A terrible waste of wool, I thought. And it occurred to me that barbed-wire and corrugated iron rendered this trepanned landscape like a First War battlefield. And that sparrow hawk – it somehow summed up Stiperstones by its slaty grey appearance, its heart-stopping yowking cry and its manner of doling out death on the wing. No wonder there were no small birds about!

The view beyond the scrubbiness of Buxton Wood, the sweep of the Shropshire plain, hazy with distance, the Breiddens and Nesscliff like a smudge, the arms of the Berwyns all-enclosing, lulled me almost out of consciousness.

'Get a move on,' a shrill voice said, 'or yo'll fall off that bike!'

It was Knucky, for all the world like Ancient Pistol, hopping along beside me like the tame jackdaw we used to have at Little Ness. He wore some old battle dress and forage cap with, yes, his campaign medal – a piece of worn-out mistletoe! He had a face like nibbled cheese. His basket was empty.

'I've jus' got one more call, an' that's my wum.'

'Where's that?'

'The Knuck.'

'That's why they call you Knucky?'

'Ah, an' 'ere we bin.'

THE NOOK was painted on the gate.

It must have been the last of the houses on the hill – except for a few deserted ones. I was struck by the neatness of the garden. It was like John Arden's in *The Golden Arrow*, I thought: full of lilac, forsythia and flowering currant, and alive with bees whose hives, like tiny white houses, stood louvred and gabled in an orchard of fruit trees, some still in bloom. But what astonished me were whole laburnum hedges showering gold.

'I've seen so many pretty gardens on the way,' I remarked.

He stood behind his gate, beaming with pride under an archway of yew, like a little khaki animal.

'An' we all keeps a pig at the back,' he chuckled; 'though we'm not supposed to kill it ourselves. We'm supposed ta take it to the abbatoyer! Owja get on with Jab the Casterater?'

'Who's Jab the Casterater?'

'Well, 'im yo've jus' bin with! 'E only giv up when 'is eyes giv out. Use'ta stick the pigs too, knowed jus' the right place, jus' above the front futt, deep in theer, them three spots wheer the Devil entered the swine. Yo cun eat ev'ry bit of a pig, yo know, bar 'is squeal!'

This information he imparted with piping voice and penetrating eye. There was something peculiar about

that eye, the one which, with tilted head, he turned on
me. It was a lighter colour than the other. It was a wall
eye, such as I had only seen before in a dog or a horse.

'Course, 'ees got religion now. Still kills 'is own
pig though. Knows it off be 'eart, yo know what I
mean? Yo seed that 'am 'angin' up? They on'y 'as their
tuthree ounces uv sugar and tay frum me. Ee-ee-ee-ee!'
He had the light-headed laugh of a jay.

'Now w'eer yo goin'?' His voice dropped an octave.

'The Devil's Chair, if I can manage it,' I said.

'Go right on up. It's a lung owd way!'

I went on up, midst crazed earth, sheep, bracken
and quietude. I passed more spoilheaps, boulders,
whinberry wires, heather clumps, bell-pits, craters
and hummocks, dotted around the miners' old engine
houses, their chimneys pointing like cannon at the sky.
Past a ruined cottage, such as Stephen in *The Golden
Arrow* had struggled to do up, I came within sight
of the Devil's Chair and the attendant frost-shattered,
quartzite grinders that successive ice-floes have failed to
wear away. I saw a dead sheep in a ruck of rushes – and
a spring; but did not drink.

I lay down on that hill and smelt the earth: that
earth that oozed with rabbits' blood and whinberry
juice and claimed the lives of people lost in the snow.

> And all is seared with trade; bleared, smeared
>   with toil,
> And wears man's smudge . . .

I felt, with Stephen Southernwood, a sense of nothing-
ness; and, with Yann in *Pêcheur d'Islande*, '*l'Immensité*'.

Consider how many men must have died in those
mines. As many as in some wars!

My mind was schooled in the sudden contradictory
moods of the psalms – praying one minute for the
peace of Jerusalem; and meting out vengeance to its
enemies the next. I could not square all that with a

God of righteousness and peace. The old sheep's bones retained in all their bareness the stark grimace of death. Where, I wondered, was the Good Shepherd then?

I wrestled, like Jacob, on that stony earth, with what I considered the restrictive conventions of work, marriage and religion. Stephen in *The Golden Arrow* would have none of them. Yann, the dark hero of *Pêcheur d'Islande*, was married to the sea. The only way one could be in control of oneself and one's destiny was, it seemed, to be continually on the move. Here, in the face of the Devil's Chair, the stillness was stifling.

'Damn you,' I cried with Stephen Southernwood. 'I can neither go nor stay!'

I must have lain there for over an hour. I was sleepy with sun and the flow of streams and a distant dreamlike drumming which I took to be the quarry machinery kibbling, swallowing and regurgitating stone.

> Begin, and cease, and then again begin,
> With tremulous cadence slow, and bring
> The eternal note of sadness in . . .

But here, all round me, were people making apparently much of life's little opportunities: I was making nothing.

I decided to go back to Lord's Hill. My thin-soled shoes were wearing through. I could not walk. I had to ride, applying the front brake almost all the time down-hill. The buzzards were still wheeling – more freely than I! But the real raptors of these hills, to my mind, were the Lords of Tankerville and Bath. They took out ore and put in bones, exhausting the flesh while making a token offering (the chapel) to the spirit. Past all those twisted, but still blossoming, hawthorns with hollows at their roots where sheep huddled from the intense sun now and, in winter, from the searing wind, I came at last to the turn for Lord's Hill. I met a bushy-eyed farmer on a grey Ferguson tractor, a collie alongside, in the steep narrow lane.

'Mechanized, are we?' I called, with no fear of being heard. 'More than in unindustrialized Little Ness!' There was more sheep's wool on the wire here than I had seen at a shearing at home. Material for birds' nests, I decided, experiencing a release of spiritual and physical energy going up hill. Another engine-house chimney with bricks missing from the base: material for human homes, I guessed.

And there at last was the chapel, not at all unattractive as Mary Webb had led me to suppose.

With a little house attached, and a graveyard round the back, it was shaded by a plantation of larch. 'Fear no more the heat of the sun,' I murmured as I walked around, trying not to step on graves, or on the daisies and anemones growing like stars in the grass.

In Loving Memory of . . . There is more love in a graveyard, I thought, than anywhere else on earth.

It was cool among the stones and trees – and so peaceful I wondered if the service was still on. I peered through a low window into the church. The little company, the 'flock', was all bowed down in prayer. My mother called it the Baptists' stoop. Indeed she had adopted it herself, in preference to 'all that High Church carry-on'.

Then everyone suddenly burst out singing. And what were they singing? Not 'Oft in Danger Oft in Woe', but 'Blessed Assurance, Jesus is Mine'. Someone playing the organ was keeping the flock together all right!

In the battle between my heart and my head, my head was overruled.

An Idyll in a Hayfield

Picture a boy in a hayfield. Picture the girl with a Kodak B who spots me live and shoots me dead.

I am alone in the hayfield, listlessly turning the swathes, trying to let the air in, trying in three days to dry out the sap which has been three months building up. The sun will only scorch the top. Underneath, coarse plantain leaves lie like spread bootlaces among the glassy waves of hay. Flat-bottomed slugs lie like excised growths in pink lint, mucilaginous and cold. Fat-bottomed frogs jump out of their skins. A toad shuffles under a stone.

I was alone in the hayfield – am alone again now. There is no one to confirm or deny that a blonde girl in a white student cap and a pretty print dress rode in like the goddess Diana and, scarcely stepping from her bicycle, took one shot with her Box Brownie, turned and, white shoes whirring, fled the field.

If I had seen a unicorn I could not have been more struck by the whiteness and brightness. Was the hair blonde or was it silver? The dress may have been light blue. The shoes were white, courtly doeskin, I should think. And the pretty little teeth – the smile, so innocently white. Her eyes were blue. And her nose – her nose was just a little pug.

I won't rush this field. She'll come again . . . I'll nurse this bit of hay. A settled spell with just a shower or two of rain is better than ferocious heat. These mares' tails in the sky may bring me luck.

Picture the boy in another hayfield, bigger and three weeks more mature. So potent to me is the smell of oil, cut grass and horse's sweat that my limbs are charged with energy more than is needed for sitting on a cutter fretting its way through summer-flowering grass. And this sprung-iron seat does nothing to keep my agitation down. One triangle remains and now a cock's tail in the grass is all there is to show how high the crop once stood. I raise the blades. Click, the knowing horses head for home.

'Is that the Cow Lane field done, then?' my mother asks at tea.

'Yes, another day or two like this and it'll be ready to turn.'

'The glass is high,' she says.

'Yes, we'll have more than enough hay this year for our few cows. The Cow Lane field's a show, and there's nobody here to see it.'

That field was our fortune. South-facing, it was favoured and fertile in spring; in summer lush with hay and ankle-deep in butter-coloured aftermath; bright emerald in autumn; the mainspring of our winter wealth. On that field you felt the heart-beat of the farm.

Generations of lads like me had cropped it and combed it, cropped it and combed it; so that at any time of the year a passer-by might be heard to say: 'My, that meadow's in good heart!' From an upstairs window, looking south, we watched the flowers come in spring: speedwell in March, cowslips in April, clover in May, and buttercups in June to match the field of the Cloth of Gold.

There courting turtle-doves spun round and fanned their white-tipped tails in June. There cuckoos looped the trees together with their ceaseless round of song. There we found the peggy whitethroat's nest in nettles very near the ground; the first dog rose and honeysuckle stitching up the hedge.

There we stumbled on big-nostrilled pigeon squabs that, belly-flopping, grounded in the seas of grass.

There the cow in oestrus burst through neighbour Bertie's fence and, strident in a sullen rage, raced off to find the bull.

There we picked cool mushrooms, white on top and pink beneath, tied in with spiders' webs on dew-wet autumn grass – the cleanest things on earth.

There, on dark November days, we carted loads of ripe manure. There I saw bald Robin Turner, filthy-handed, take his teeth out, tongue them round and put them back.

And there, this early July day, I counted on the mares' tails in the sky to bring me . . . what, I was not sure – but something more than hay.

'I would like some more tomatoes from the Herb Farm,' said my mother, interrupting my thoughts. 'Not yellow ones!'

'Right, I'll go down on my bike.' I needed no telling twice.

Originally the old Pump House at Valeswood, the Herb Farm was now one of the most interesting places to go – and its present owner, Mrs Kay, one of the most cultivated ladies in the neighbourhood, whom it was always a delight to meet. She surrounded herself with mystery. She spoke in a hushed contralto voice: indeed, her speech was more like song, decorated now and again with an idiom from another language – German, Italian, French. She fixed long Latin names to her plants though to many of the villagers she seemed to grow only weeds.

'Them poppies,' they asked, 'am they fer opium, d'ya think?'

The silk-worms munched away on mulberry leaves. She dried all sorts of things in over-heated old tin sheds. Lavender was one. She talked sotto voce in a steamed-up greenhouse while helping me to pounds of pungent, ripe tomatoes: 'Try the yellow ones,' she said. 'They're every bit as good. People are so prejudiced; they think raspberries and tomatoes all have to be red. They don't mind plums being yellow. How's the Italian?'

I was learning Italian with a bit of help from Mrs Kay. I was attracted to it by Mozart – whose name she pronounced Modz-art.

'What does *Così Fan Tutte* mean?' I asked her, trying a yellow tomato.

'Cosi Fan Too-tay,' she crooned. 'It's impossible to translate. Something like, women are all the same – which you know to be false.'

Before spraying the greenhouse again or gathering fresh fodder for the insatiable silk-worms, she took me into the parlour. She sank contentedly in a shapeless settee and I sat in an armchair by a bookcase bulging with botany.

'I suppose botany is your consuming passion,' I said.

'No,' she replied. 'Alfic, my husband, is my consuming passion. How did you like Lisbet?'

'Ah,' I twigged. 'The girl with the camera. You knew about that?'

'She's staying with me. She's Danish – daughter of

an old friend I met at finishing school in Switzerland. She came back very starry-eyed!'

Did she mean Lisbet, or the friend from finishing school?

'Where is she now – I mean Lisbet,' I asked, expecting to be told she'd gone back.

'Picking beans at the far end of the top field. I won't let her out until after tea.'

'Can I go and help?'

'No, you can go home with your tomatoes and get on with your *Piccolo Mondo Antico*.'

Mrs Kay's tomatoes tasted delicious at tea that day. Pity those greenhouses were so steamed up and those corrugated drying sheds stood between the house and the field where Lisbet worked. I might have snapped a glimpse of her – or she of me . . .

'Don't gulp your tea down so fast,' my mother said. 'The hay can wait.' I tended to agree; but only in the long term. I'd done the milking and was more than eager to start turning the bottom end of the field where, in the shadow of a high hawthorn hedge, the hay took longer to dry.

So, pitch-fork in hand, I went, feet swishing through the swathes. A little shower had brought fresh fragrance to the field. A thrush sang in the Cow Lane oak. Purple vetch and clover stained the flesh wounds of the field, but a little group of harebells still shivered in safety on an uncut knoll.

'Calm was the day, and through the trembling air sweet-breathing Zephyrus did play . . . ' The pitch-fork jerked in my hand like a water-diviner's rod. It was Lisbet; her white student cap was bobbing up the lane.

'A gentle spirit,' I rejoined, 'that lightly did delay hot Titan's beams, which then did glister fair!'

'Good day,' she called, in an arch and foreign way. But the smile was natural enough. 'You are too much in the shade for me to see.'

'Good, then you can't take a photograph!' I stabbed the pikel in the ground and strolled towards the sunlit lane.

'You like Spenser?'

'Yes, so very much. I studied him at school.'

'School is over? So what are you going to do now?'

'Become a dentist. See where the practice-drill caught a hold of my hair.'

She removed her little white student cap, revealing a scar and a tuft of hair growing like a fringe, but upwards. It was as if it were on a spring. The sun emphasized what I had noticed before: her hair was more like silver than gold. Platinum was too metallic a word. It was like the sheen that you sometimes see when the sun falls low on a lake of hay.

Her skin was too fair to take a tan; but there was a hint of cream on her upper arm – honeysuckle cream, tinted with rose, that set off the style of her blue-ribboned dress. And the most remarkable thing was that her dress went down to only a foot above the ankle.

'Do you like the new look?' she asked. 'Yes?' And she twirled around.

'I do.'

'You play the piano?'

'A bit,' I admitted.

'More than a bit, Mrs Kay tells me; I play the cello,' she added and was halfway back down the lane to fetch it. What could a man do? I picked a late rose from the hedge and strolled back to the house.

'Going to practise the piano, Mum. I think I might need to.'

I put the rose in a little vase on the piano as if it had been there all the time. A petal dropped, and then another. No help. I was trying too hard.

Mother was topping and tailing gooseberries on the sunlit porch; doing them almost, it seemed, in her sleep.

We always kept open house, and on a fine July evening it was no surprise to Mother when Lisbet walked in. She was perhaps a little wistful at the sight of the cello – which her father used to play – but when Lisbet offered to help with the gooseberries all sense of strangeness passed away.

'I do them for Mrs Kay,' she said amiably. 'Have you a scissors?' I found a pair in the kitchen drawer.

'See!' She was snipping away in her new-fangled fashion while Mother worked on them deftly with her hands.

When Lisbet told her how many beans she had pulled and podded that day she said, 'Go and relax with the cello. I shall enjoy hearing it out here.'

Lisbet had just spent a few days in Wales which she said was 'so beautiful'. She had found a little book of folk songs containing 'Watching the Wheat' – *'Bugeilio'r Gwenith Gwyn'*. I made a harp-like accompaniment from the guitar chords provided and Lisbet played the melody with broad, firm sweeps of the bow. She had a lovely bowing arm and a dreaming sway of the head that drew attention to her shining eyes and hair. And as we played we sang:

> 'Idle days in summer time,
>   in pleasant summer weather,
> Amid the golden coloured corn
>   two lovers passed together;
> Many words they did not speak
>   to give their thoughts expression –
> Each knew the other's heart was full,
>   and neither made confession.'

We played *'Dafydd y Gareg Wen'* and *'Ei Di'r Du'*. We skipped over *'I wisgo aur-goron'* (in English, 'Be Merry but Wise').

'What beautiful names!' Lisbet said, regardless of their

sense. We scrambled through 'Counting the Goats', twisting our tongues and our insides with laughter. But we came back to *'Bugeilio'r Gwenith Gwyn'*.

'If Mrs Kay doesn't let you out till after tea, what time do you have to be in?'

'Oh, I don't have to be in!' She put her cello in its case and put her arms round me.

'My beloved is white and ruddy, the chiefest among ten thousand. His head is as the most fine gold, his locks are bushy, and black as a raven . . . '

Did I know the Song of Solomon? I did, but not by heart.

'How do you know Spenser and the Song of Solomon?' I asked. 'And in English?'

'How else would I know them?' she pouted prettily. 'They don't sound so good in Danish.'

'Say something in Danish.'

'Jeg elsker deg.'

'I know that,' I said. I turned from the piano and, picking up the cello case, made for the door.

'May I leave it here?' she asked.

'Of course,' I said.

'With all my heart,' she added winsomely.

'Sounded very nice to me,' said Mother, when Lisbet had gone. 'She's a pretty little thing. I like her dress. Longer styles are coming in.'

'And longer shadows, too,' I might have added – or 'ichabod', if I had known the word.

Already the nights were drawing in. It was surprising, I always thought, how soon after midsummer day a heaviness lay on the evening air and the dew no longer drew forth the sweeter scents of wild rose, hay and clover but the coarser ones of hogweed, sow-thistle, woundwort and dock. I should have to clear a path through the nettles in the stackyard which leaned out at you, grabbed you by the ear and filled your nose with their hot, rank breath. You could even catch the smell of iodine from the walnuts ripening past the stage when they were at their best for pickling, when their shells began to harden and their jackets swell, then spot with black, then rot and start to fall away. Soon it would be winter again, and we would crack them round the fire, some black as a decaying tooth, some creamy-white inside their crinkled, skull-like hemispheres.

I knew that Mother sensed my restlessness. I 'mooned about' too much. I hadn't a lot to do apart from the hay, and I had decided not to hurry over that. This was not the life for me, I thought; well, not for long. We kept only a few cows now and a couple of dozen hens and my old bantams for a regular income of cash.

'Why don't you take your bike and show Lisbet around tomorrow?'

'Thanks, Mum,' I said. 'She'd like that.'

'If you can get her away from the bean-pods.'

So next day we whistled round Wales; the parts that border the Breidden, beyond Llanymynech and Llansantffraid. We were not sure how to say Llanfyllin, but we were sure it could not be 'Clan-fill-in'. We sang 'Watching the Wheat' and our bicycle spokes sparkled, spinning in the sun. We joined our hands as naturally as we joined our voices. We saw a canal and a railway running over a river; a road, a railway and a canal running side by side; but never a road, a river, a canal and a railway all together. We had lunch at a pub, though we both looked under-age. Above the village of Llanfechain which, I told Lisbet, was Topsy's birthplace, we lay on a sun-baked hill.

'Your girl friend?' she asked.

'My Welsh mountain pony,' I said.

'There's a Welsh mountain chicken,' she joked.

'And a Welsh rarebit,' I laughed, not looking at the rabbit, but her. With my fingertip I traced the tiny sprigs of thyme in the short, sheep-bitten turf. She lay on her back in an open-eyed dream while I watched and wondered and mentally explored her body smelling of sun and spice.

'There are no rabbits in Denmark – only hares,' she said.

I was tired of word-play.

'Tell me *all* about Denmark,' I said.

She told me about the palaces and castles – Fredensborg, Christiansborg, Rosenborg and Elsinore; about the gay lights and fountains and the amusements in the gardens at Tivoli.

'What about Danish music?' I asked. 'Is there any?'

'Yes,' she said sternly. 'We have Nielsen – you know his *Fynsk Foraar*?'

'His what?'

'*Springtime in Funen*. He also has written his *Childhood on Funen*. We have the conductor Mogens Woldike, and our King conducts the Danish Radio Symphony Orchestra sometimes.'

'And art?'

'Thorvaldsen. You never heard of Thorvaldsen?'

I, child-like, held a buttercup under her chin to see if she liked butter and made some foolish remark about my little Danish dairymaid. It was then that I saw the cloud roll over Lisbet's sunny face.

'The Fates,' she said. 'D'you know the Fates? Clotho who spins the threads of life; Lachesis who apportions our lots; and Atropos who cuts the threads with a sword.'

'I have so far managed to live in happy ignorance of those interfering busybodies,' I said.

'Oh, you are so *yong*!' She put on her strong Teutonic look. 'The grass of the field that today is and tomorrow is cast into the oven.'

'Exactly,' I said. 'So take no thought for the morrow. Shall he not clothe you, O ye of little faith?'

But my mocking had the wrong effect. She was serious. Suddenly I could no longer make her smile; and she, being under a cloud, put me under one too – as dark as the cloud shadows on the hills. I wished that ours, like theirs, would shift. And soon!

I pointed at long-tailed bully-boy lambs butting under their mothers so forcefully they lifted them off their thin hind legs. Lisbet thought the ewes with horns were rams.

'See,' I said, putting her cap on the head of one that came up to question our identity, 'she's one of us!'

'Speak for yourself,' said Lisbet, and ran bare-footed after the giddy, blindfold ewe.

'Come on,' I said. 'Let's go to Llanrhaeadr.' We went through the beautiful valley of the Tanat. We were not far, Lisbet said, from Owen Glendower's castle at Sycharth. She had read about this in George Borrow's *Wild Wales*. What hadn't she read? And she knew about the Ladies of Llangollen and Dinas Bran – as high, she said, as the highest hill in Denmark. It was easy to see why she found Wales so romantic.

'There,' she said. 'The one unbroken thread of life!' She may have been thinking of Borrow's attempts to describe the waterfall: an immense skein of silk, agitated and disturbed by tempestuous blasts; the long tail of a grey courser at furious speed.

We saw the house where he was given a bowl of buttermilk; the birthplace, as it happened – though I did not think of it then – of Ellen, my mother's old friend, whom we called Auntie Nell.

I had been to Rhyl on the train. I had been to Berriew once, but only at night to see an English play. I did not know Welshpool. The Breidden was still my western frontier; the point where the sun went down. It was my little Danish 'dairymaid' who introduced me to the real character of the 'foreign country' that lay beyond.

The next day, Lisbet brought a message from Mrs Kay. Why don't we go to the show?

'What show?'

'The flower show.'

I had never been to the flower show; *Shrewsbury Musical and Floral Fête*, as it was billed. As small children we had always gone to the Shropshire and West Midland Show across the river. It was a cheap day out. The bus dropped us at Frankwell and we boarded the ferry, my brother, my two sisters, my Mam and cow-licked me. We had free tickets for meals at Bibby's tent. The Severn seemed as wide as the Mississippi as the ferryman hauled on the groaning rope and the flat-bottomed craft exchanged one comfortable berth in a reed-bed for another.

'You keep with me,' our mother yelled. We clattered through the turnstiles and clomped about on duck-boards, past the sideshows, till we reached the main arena.

'Agincourt!' my brother cried. 'The tents, the flags, the horses – all stirred by the wind!' Men in hard hats and badges pointed shooting sticks like guns; and stockmen in their fluttering smocks grew grim and small as they strained to hold masked bulls with sticks and chains.

''*Tiser!*' shouted the *Advertiser* man. 'Programmes! *Ev'nin' Echo!* All the ring events!'

We took our places for the Grand Parade, smelling of sweat and sun-burnt straw and grass and dung. We had six lumps of sugar in our tea when we crowded into Bibby's tent. We watched the farriers at their vulcan forges and smelt of smelted iron afterwards; of smoke and tarry horses' hooves.

And then we haunted pens where proud men slept in broad daylight, their past rosettes pinned up on lids of open trunks, their present ones displayed along the stalls and on the heads of beasts that looked like princes and princesses, unconcerned about the madding crowd. The Flower Show? Well, that was expensive – and exclusive.

'I've never been to the Flower Show.'

'Well, now's your chance for a wisit.'

'I can't go till after milking.'

'That's all right. There's all night after that. I'll put my bike in the back of the Crate' – the name we gave to Mrs Kay's old timber-sided station waggon. 'We'll cycle home together.'

'Won't you be tired – I mean, after being there all day?'

'Me, tired? I never tire. At Tivoli I've been on the figure eight twenty-two times. Torben betted me I would be sick. All right? Oh, in your lazy afternoon – your *après-midi d'un faune* – you can read this.' She slid a book in a brown-paper cover under my arm, bobbed up and planted a kiss on my right ear. '*Kitty Foyle*. Make hay while the sun shines, dear!' I grinned and she bowled bob-billowing away.

Kitty Foyle first appears knickerless in her Mid-west hometown, goes to 'Chicawgo', has a back-street abortion, then moves to New York where she keeps her head but loses most everything else. A smart cookie, very funny – but not my type. I wondered all through the evening milk why Lisbet had given it me to read . . .

I rushed my tea, washed, cleaned my teeth – something my mother said I never did – plastered Brylcreem on my hair and wore my Hepworth's suit.

'You look like a shop-walker,' Mother said.

'Hello!' I said with a man-of-the-world's assurance when I met Mrs Kay, seated beside an elderly lady I didn't know. Lisbet was standing next to them grinning like a Cheshire cat. The elderly lady averted her gaze. Mrs Kay seemed unaccountably embarrassed.

'You're late,' said Lisbet, taking my arm and marching me off. 'I want a drink!'

The showground extended, it seemed, throughout the Quarry park. There was show-jumping down by the river and marquees were massed about the Dingle, up to St Chad's, the bandstand and Town Walls. A man was leaping from a pylon into a bath of fire. I wanted to see the show-jumping.

'We might see Pat Smythe,' I said.

'Pat who?'

'Pat Smythe.'

'Who's he?' It was clear my little Lisbet did not follow sport.

We dragged ourselves round hot and airless tents with grand, exotic blooms — too gaudy to be gay, too sickly-scented to refresh.

'I want a *drink!*' My arm was being pulled from its socket.

'And so do I!' I snapped. She moved away. 'There are no drinks.'

'There must be somewhere.'

'Yes, but somewhere isn't here.'

We passed the rose tent. Harry Wheatcroft appeared, bow-tied, with bushes on his cheeks and a rambler of a moustache. We laughed at the names: Mrs Sam McGredy, Minnehaha, Miss Edith Cavell, Nypel's Perfections, Polly . . . And then we found the beer. And a queue about a mile long.

'It doesn't open till six,' I said. The heat was overpowering. There was no air in the Quarry. It was like a dust-bowl after two days of people trampling the dried-out, polished grass. You could hardly keep on your feet.

'By God, it's a scorcher,' said a man in a tweed suit and matching cap. 'I'd take my jacket off, only for my braces.'

'Only for his braces?' Lisbet whispered.

'Ssh!'

'Have you got braces?'

'No.'

'Then take your jacket off.'

'And you carry it?'

I took it off. Dark pools of perspiration which had started under my armpits now spread halfway round my back.

'You're sweeting,' Lisbet said. She didn't make many mistakes, but this was one.

'Sweating,' I corrected her.

'OK. You should use talc. Have you heard of Amplex?'

At last we reached the trestle tables, the lengths of which were stacked with crates of beer.

'Pale ale or Worthington's?' I never drank beer but now I was ready for anything. 'Or cider?'

'Cider, yes!' said Lisbet, jumping up and down.

'Two ciders, please.'

Two ciders we had. Woodpecker, straight from the bottle: huge, black bottles, heavy, thick and thumping to the teeth.

'We'd best sit down to this,' I said. We spread my jacket out. I caught the strains of 'Country Gardens' coming from the bandstand; the beat boomed in the earth: *boom boom, tra la-la, boom boom, tralee; boom boom boom boom – boom di boom.*

'Rose white and lily, pinks and sweet willy, the country gardens come to town.'

'What a rich deep voice you have, just like Paul Robeson.'

'Oh, thank you,' I purred.

'And lips to match.' She put her finger on my bottom lip and spread it out. 'And nice white teeth.'

'You're teasing me.'

'Of course. It's the woman's privilege to tease.'

'And the man's to tell the truth?'

'Yes, I suppose.'

The band played on: 'Just the Way You Look Tonight', 'An English Rose' . . .

'Dan Cupid hath a garden,' I sang, 'where women are the flowers . . . '

'Write a poem – *hick* – about a rose,' Lisbet laughed, half-mockingly. 'A perfect Eenglish rose.'

I was too far gone with cider, scent and sun. An evening breeze played round my open shirt. The band droned on and voices mingled, came and went. Skirts and ankles, trouser turn-ups, plus-fours and shooting sticks passed by my head. The milling throng. I felt a boldness I had never felt before – a safety in the crowd. We drowsed and swooned together, sweat with sweat and sweet with sweet; wrapped up, one might say, in ourselves.

We must have cycled home. I would have remembered if we had walked. No matter. The night was young and warm.

Only next day did I know in how many ways I had disgraced myself. Lisbet was asked to be very particular to tell me that one did not address oneself to strangers with familiar greetings like hello; that in Denmark couples who were seen arm in arm were assumed to be engaged; and, as if for good measure, she threw in my rendering of 'Dan Cupid hath a garden' which was, she said, maudlin and flat.

The barometer was falling. I had to get on with the hay, forking it – where ready – into cocks. Lisbet came bouncing in wearing another new-look dress. She said she had been unable to sleep for excitement, so she had copied out all she could remember of Spenser's *Epithalamion*.

'But did you see the dawn?' she asked. I had to confess I did not. 'I sleep, but my heart waketh . . .

Behold thou art fair, my beloved, yea, pleasant,' she said: 'also our bed is green . . . '

We stayed in again that night, playing and singing our favourite songs but not '*Bugeilio'r Gwenith Gwyn*'. The second verse was sad with the parting of the lovers.

It was Mrs Kay who had told me that Lisbet would be going back to Denmark in two days' time. I flew to Shrewsbury to the jeweller's and there found a silver bracelet which I thought would look well on her lovely bowing arm.

She came to tea the last evening and I saw Mother look wistfully again as the cello was put in its case for the last time.

'There is one piece I wish you would play, Lisbet – *The Swan*.' She had seen Pavlova dance it many years before.

I found the piano part taxing, so stiff and sore were my stumbling hands, but Lisbet loaded her long melodic lines with gold. It seemed to me that she played it extra well, in tribute to my mother's trust, her intuition that this girl who knew Spenser and the Song of Songs – and yet was going to be a dentist – was herself a source of pure and exquisite delight.

She was leaving by the Harwich–Esbjerg ferry the next day. I would not be able to see her off because of the milking and the hay, which, by now, was ready to be stacked. It seemed the best time to give Lisbet the bracelet.

'Set me a seal upon thine arm,' I said.

'For love is strong as death,' said Lisbet.

'Many waters cannot quench love,' said my mother.

Lisbet gave me her picture – the one she had taken of me that first day in the hayfield. I looked like a dusky, black-haired Greek.

'Where', I asked, 'is my flock of goats?' And on her copy I wrote what she had written on mine: *Jeg elsker deg*. – I love you.

Never a Bird in a Cage

'We let our girls do the fighting,' my brother once observed. 'The boys stayed at home.'

Laura had voluntarily exchanged her Land Army breeches and jacket for the skirt and tunic of the ATS. And Belle was in the WRNS: she liked the uniform. John was undergoing 'industrial experience'; 'tinkering with radar in the distant Malvern Hills', as Mother described it. He was also studying English Literature.

Conscription being still in force, my Priory friends had all left home: Martin killing time as an army education officer and Kite cleaning out latrines. Only Dickie was actually flying. And there was, of course, no fighting. They were in some uncertain way preserving the peace. I, even I only, was left – in a more uncertain way trying to secure the future of the farm. Unconscripted, unconstrained, I read *Tess of the d'Urbervilles* and *Jude the Obscure* and kept myself to myself, living like a dragonfly nymph at the bottom of a deep and muddy pond.

But I worked at my music. Oh, how I worked! I had read that Sir Charles Hallé practised so hard when he was young that his wrists swelled up like footballs. I would do the same. The Bechstein would buckle before I bowed! The Revolutionary Study rattled the shutters of the Empty Room; the Winter Wind banged on the windowpanes.

Faithful Penny could always find me there. She had become a part of my life – this staunch, stand-offish, no-come-hither girl. She came in to listen, leaning on her elbows and standing with her legs apart.

'Why don't you sit down?' I used to ask.

'I'm not staying long,' she always replied. But she did. She hung around the cowhouse door. I squirted her with milk. She watched me picking plums. I dropped them on her head . . .

And, prompt on cue, in lovely low September light, came Flather on his damson run. *Flather & Waddington, Halifax*, gold letters on the lorry said. But only Mr Flather came. I heard his lorry throbbing by the gate. A cough, out stepped the heavy man on nimble little feet. The door shut with a bang, he touched his hat, a smile lit up his unbrimmed eye.

'Ow bist?' he said.

He thumbed his braces, eyed the fruit.

'Is that the lot?' He gave a thoughtful pull at the sight of two clothes baskets full of ruby-purple plums.

'Ah'll tak the lot – a pound a strike.'

I did the work; he mopped his brow.

'Ah'll tak the lot. Get t'steel yard oot!' I weighed the crop.

'Two strike – or nigh enoof.' He lifted his hat and wiped his face and opened up a wad of notes and, slowly counting, gave me two.

Two pounds for all that work! I was lucky if I picked a strike (that's ninety pounds) in a day. Dust and specks of wood got in my eyes and round my waist

inside my shirt. My shins and feet and shoulders ached
from standing rigid on my rickety gap-runged ladder.
If something cracked I froze; and damson boughs
crack suddenly. The boughs – snagged with thorns and
closely set – are difficult to climb. One Saturday morning, emboldened by the sunshine, I left the ladder, my
bucket and bacon-hook swinging from a distant rung,
and struggled up among the mazy canopy, kicking
against the pricks, until I stood unsteady at the top.

'Plenty of fruit! Forbidden! Out of reach!' I yelled
to Penny below.

Crack! The fickle damson bough snapped clean away;
but I was held by an intermediate spar, gripping and
rending the seat of my trousers and scoring my skin.

How to get past Penny? I lingered in pain. I felt a
trickle down my leg of sweat and blood . . . I put my
finger on the spot and felt the stickiness.

'I've struck a sticky patch,' I grinned through gritted
teeth. Unmoved, the girl remained. I loosed my grip
and landed in a heap. No movement still. The wind,
though light, puffed rudely through the rent in my
backside. It's huge, I thought; and walked, ridiculously,
backwards to the house. And opened up the gap. And
closed the door.

'A letter for you,' my mother said. 'You'd better
wash your hands.'

Hardly stopping to examine the small, regular, royal-
blue handwriting, I jagged open the envelope – fragrant
and blue with tissue-paper lining to match.

'Mind the stamp! And go upstairs and take those
trousers off and—'

'And don't forget to wash your hands . . . ' I finished
the sentence for her, already half-way to my room.

'The water's down here!' she called after me.

I never washed or changed so quickly, or for such

a good reason. The letter was as funny as it was fragrant.

I went on the *King of Denmark* [Lisbet wrote] and I came back on the *Queen*. If anything the *Queen* was rougher than the *King*. But after Liverpool Street and the desolation of Harwich she was like a white and gold palace, painted and poised on the water. It was five o'clock in the evening, eating time. I went below for a cup of tea. I suddenly found that I could not eat. I was choked – full up, you say?

In about an hour the bars were opened and the ship came to life. The smell of cooking mounted to the deck. The drawl of Southern English voices gave way to snatches of Danish, German and Dutch. (Is that a language? Ugh!) There was a grinding of hausers, a churning of harbour water like beer boiling round the hull and a sudden absence of conversation. The seagulls took up the chant. The ship turned (I thought the wrong way) righted itself and slowly steamed into the Western Sea. (You call it the North Sea.) Conversation bubbled up again, but I was alone, stabbed by the whiteness of the cliffs as the ship left a wake of sun-lit silver and the cooks threw empty boxes on the water for the seagulls to complain about.

When you come over here please don't be sick – what happened to me. The saloons were full of cigar-smoking, beer-swilling Nord Friesischers and Schleswig-Holsteins and *Dutch*! I bought a sandwich and went back up on deck. My fellow passengers were all camped and organized. Their sleeping-bags unrolled, they had souwesters keeping out the draught. And what a draught! I only had on my student cap!

I must have sleeped a little, but not so well as the organized ones. Even they had to get up from time to time to unstiff their joints by prowling moodily around the deck. I finally curled up on a couch in the

saloon and cat-napped, clutching my case. A clatter of
cutlery, a noticeable increase of Danish and I snapped
myself awake, fearing I had slept too long.

My stomach was knotted up and I was paralysed
with cold. I was walled in with stale tobacco smoke.
With furry tongue, stiff neck and aching bottom
bones, my eyes feeling as if matches had been struck
behind the balls, I heaved myself and my case away.
I tottered past a waiter balancing a tray shoulder-high
with plates of greasy pop-eyed eggs. I was immedi-
ately overcome and showered with warm and bitter
bile and tea. Another steward, with perfect timing,
gave me his starched white napkin and helped me to
a seat. Tears scalded my cheeks but my whole body
was cold. I put the napkin to my eyes and caught its
crisp, clean laundered smell. 'Don't worry,' he said,
'there's some worse sick than you. Those terrible
English with their bacon and eggs!'

The letter ended:

You must read *Brand*. Ibsen is better than Shaw. I
send you a message down a moonbeam. *Jeg elsker
deg*. I am in the arms of Morpheus. Good night.

I had never had to reckon before with the force of
love's sickness. Letters poured in from København's
Beringsvej.

John wrote by the week from Malvern: had I read
Screwtape? What did I think of *The Prelude* and Harold
Nicolson's masterly reports from the United Nations
on the Third Programme?

Martin wanted to know if I had finished *Mr Weston's
Good Wine*. He was caught up in *The Quest for Corvo*.
Dickie wrote, sometimes twice a week, from Bridgnorth on the prospect of flying in Rhodesia, soaring
over the veldt. What must it be like in a Spitfire over

the Victoria Falls, blue sky above, blue lake and rolling cloud below? He had his wings. Our pens could not keep up with the excitement.

But Lisbet wrote by the day – by the hour, it seemed. Had I read *Brand*? She sent me a little book of Danish poems: *In Denmark I Was Born*, Danish on one side, English on the other. 'Now you will learn Danish.' I learnt what I thought were the names of some wild flowers – and *jeg elsker deg*. Messages of love came on moonbeams. 'I send you a kiss on a moonbeam.'

Lisbet's style was as pretty and neat as her person: unwavering, controlled, set firmly between the margins, as lyrically blue as her new-look dress. Sometimes she came in pink (paper, that is); still fragrant as a flower: but then I knew the moon had been temporarily dismissed and Phoebus and his chariot engaged.

Wake, now my love, awake; for it is time,
The Rosy Morne long since left Tithone's bed . . .

'And what does Lisbet have to say?' my mother sometimes asked, impaling corn-bills on a spike.
'She wants me to go next summer.'
'Where?'
'Denmark.'
'And with what?'

If Mother had said 'What on?' I could have answered 'Bicycle.' Lisbet was always proposing riding round Denmark together, much as we had ridden, singing, holding hands or trailing tuneful grass stems in our rear-wheel spokes round Wales.

'But that was only for a day, and one small part of Wales,' my mother pointed out. 'Denmark is all islands – and disconnections. You'd have to take ferries and sleep on deck and . . . '

'We can stay with the aunts. And her grandfather lives at Vejle. He has over a hundred pipes, she says. And he's very musical.'

'Your grandfather was very musical too,' she said.

I did not tell her that Lisbet also proposed staying in hotels. The one at Silkeborg was very good. We could take a boat on the lake. No one would see us. The reeds grew high . . .

'It's very pretty in summer, I'm sure.' My mother called my wandering attention back.

'Yes. Lisbet says the churches are small, white and sinless.' (I don't know how she came to choose that word.) 'And the houses generally prettier than ours; shingle and weather-boarded, white or natural wood, with graceful sweeping curved tiled roofs.'

'Yes, I remember her saying our council houses are all alike, all straight and dull and institutional.'

'We might see *Hamlet* at Helsingør.' More pause for thought.

'She has a step-father, hasn't she?'

'Yes, but I expect he's all right.'

'I'm sure.' She said it as if she were not. 'Ah, well. I never wanted to be a bird in a cage. You go.'

Mother had mellowed. And, just to make her laugh, I reminded her how Lisbet had once told us she loved going round the aunts who were dispersed all over Denmark and were so hospitable and always ready to welcome you, 'their big bowels full of sour cream'.

'*Chacun à son goût*,' my mother crashed through her burnt toast. 'You'd better get on.' She meant with the work.

Yes, Mother had mellowed. There were no moonbeams in her life; but she had come to terms with the irksome drudgery of an old farmhouse. For long years she had spat resentment in a song: 'I believe in doing what I can', from *Bitter Sweet*. It went with the vim

and vigour with which she tackled – and had us tackle
– the hardest tasks.

'. . . in crying when I must, in laughing when
I choose. Heigho – ' She had a talent to amuse.

Now she had settled into a mould, all edges
smoothed, as physically comfortable as she would
ever be. She was a mistress of economy. To see
her peel an apple in one long coil of green was an
ever-fresh delight. The smoothing iron went smoother
over the sheets, now there were fewer sheets to do. The
bucket grated less on the kitchen floor as she swung the
floor-cloth in wide arcs of shining wetness, clouding
in the sunlight back to terracotta warmth: if I would
only leave my wellingtons outside. The darning needle
skipped between the warp and weft on heels of socks,
now there were fewer socks to darn. The pen sizzled
over the paper in a race to catch the evening post. She
always used a Waverley nib. Her letters were long,
assured and – as I found out after I left home – extremely
fine. I should have kept them all. She observed more of
life from her small cell than many, of less humour, did
from better vantage points.

Her problems had for over twenty years been large-
ly economic. Now she was able to keep them at arm's
length – as she did her bank account: at Hoylake, where
it had always been, a hundred miles away.

She cooked on the fire or on an old oil-stove.
What need had she of printed recipes? They were all
in her head. What need of electricity? She read in bed
by candlelight. She had become defensive of the inertia
that sets in after the fray.

Our lives were still held in orbit by the Church's year.
There were still the time-honoured physical signs of the
seasons: rooks at Candlemas beginning to build their
nests: Lammas plums; the Michaelmas goose. Only,
thank God, we did not kill the pig at Martinmas. People
died; and not too many babies were born. There were

110

never to be corridors and dark passageways echoing to the thrill of Sardines and Murder again. Pieces of our small, tight-fitting jigsaw moved, or were lost. The bell tolled for old retainers at 'The House' as Mrs Darby's door remained increasingly tight shut. John, the waggoner's lad, followed the horses into the twilight, edged out as fancied Fordsons filled the fields. A small tributary, the Perry, still tinkled on its apparently timeless way through lands once torn by border feuds to join the flowing river, on to reach the seas of change . . .

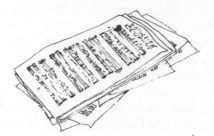

A Spreading of Wings

'Twas on the Isle of Capri that I found her
Beneath the shade of an old walnut tree
Oh! I can still see the flowers blooming round her
Where we met on the Isle of Capri.
She was as sweet as a rose at the dawning
But somehow fate hadn't meant her for me
And tho' I sailed with the tide in the morning
Still my heart's in the Isle of Capri.

'The Isle of Capri' had come to Little Ness as early as 1934. It had come in the same way as 'Poor Little Angeline', 'Hometown', 'Red Sails in the Sunset' and 'Roll Along Covered Wagon'. My music-loving mum had brought it home, seven and a half miles from Shrewsbury, on a Saturday night. She had mused over it on the bus; then, still in her fur coat and smelling of unfamiliar scent, she had played it over on the piano and we had sung 'la-la-la-la, over Naples bay. That's where my thoughts keep on turning, la-la-la-la. Where romance came to me . . . ' – our breaths condensing in the Empty Room till the candles guttered in their

112

brackets and blobs of wax congealed like pig's lard on the yellowing ivories. Indeed the Empty Room smelt as damp and unused as the larder where the killed pig lay and a struck match stung the nerve-endings of your frozen nose.

But somehow 'The Isle of Capri' was more than the ordinary roll-along-covered-wagon song, or 'Little Old Lady Passing By'. She, of the plain golden ring on her finger who whispered softly 'It's best not to linger', spoke to us of romance, of soft Italian eyes, the Mediterranean, of what might have been . . .

Was it the old walnut tree familiarly set between our stackyard and the orchard that so vividly fixed the scene for me? Thirteen years later, in 1947, instead of heeding fate and the sultry sibilant warning of the song I was positively emboldened by those words. I sailed with the tide in the morning – not home like the sailor, but out across the Naples bay, with 'Lady I'm a rover' beating on my unsettled adolescent voice and in my pullulating heart.

I sang as I followed the cows up the road, taking them to their pasture in the parsonage field. If I had not sung, the parson might have missed his breakfast, a perfectly timed and lightly-set boiled egg; the schoolmistress might not have remembered to ring the bell for the beginning of school at nine o'clock.

'Summer time was nearly over,' I cried to the startled rooks in the parsonage trees. After me, John the waggoner's lad might rumble by with a cart to fetch turnips, singing 'Roll me over in the clover, roll me over, lay me down and do it again.' Or the muck spreaders grumble by with 'The wheel of the waggon is broken an' it ain't goin' to turn no more; the old grey mare is dead an' gone . . . '

'Not yet, she isn't!' John would shout. It was all wishful thinking – all in defiance of Bill Whitefoot who stood up off the tractor seat and roared through the village with no time for singing and no time for romance . . .

It was Martin who told me about *Sons and Lovers*: Martin who preferred the music of the spheres to that of the milking pail; who identified himself (and you) with characters in books; who impersonated the husky Marlene Dietrich and the strident Gracie Fields; who spoke of Emma Woodhouse and Elizabeth Bennet as if they were his friends and called Princess Elizabeth 'Betty, the suet pudding that needs a stir'.

After leaving school I kept in touch with all my Priory friends: Dickie, the indelible best; Maurice who had moved to Manchester and had turned Janeite, scribe and Hallé concert-goer and now wrote long and exquisitely wrought epistles from fog-bound Bramhall Lane. Then there was the elegant loafer, Kite. And now Martin, the mocking grand illusionist from Weston Lullingfields.

How Little Ness had changed since the war! This was a topic I often discussed with Martin, an observer – indeed in one sense, an agent – of change.

From being almost entirely a community of sons of the soil we had acquired what is now termed a good social mix. The Reverend Eaton Evans had come here to retire. He was one of Martin's friends; tall and absent-minded – but not so much that when he saw a gate that I had left open onto the road he did not close it 'to avert an accident'. Then there were the evacuees who had chosen to stay, like the perambulating Pettigrews. (Mrs Pettigrew pushed the pram and smoked perpetually. It ran on smoke, my mother said.) There were also the shadowy Raeders who, my brother said, were really internees. They walked and clutched their feathery, pop-eyed Papillon dogs and scooped up horse muck from the road with a trowel, a coal-scuttle and delicately gloved hands. They had strange names and mystifying purposes.

And there was Mrs Kay: she who grew marjoram,

chamomile, bergamot and rue; lavender, rosemary and
– what looked like daisies – feverfew. And, oh dear,
those yellow tomatoes! But it was a treat to stand in
her hot tomato houses and smell the sun-soaked fruit,
and listen to Mrs Kay say rue with a Mediterranean
accent; to see the smile in her Mediterranean blue eyes.
And to be led by the ear to the shed where silk-worms
worked on piles of leaves from the parson's mulberry
tree. They chomped around the edges with alarming
rapidity and greed. I did not know what 'chamfered'
meant but tried it out.

'Ah, *le mot juste!*' she cried. She spread out her
hands and spread out her teeth and her socks fell
in rucks round her feet.

So, with Mrs Kay, the Bowles, the Pettigrews and
the Raeders, the village mix had been transformed and
Martin was there to give it a stir.

'This village is full of Miriams languishing with
their hens.'

'More like frustrated Pauls,' said I.

I responded to the natural, homely elements in the
book which reflected, however obliquely, some of my
own experience. I liked the collier kitchen scenes: Paul
washing his father's back (I remembered washing my
father's back when he was frail; how smooth it was
compared with his gouged-out wounded arm). And
the Levers' kitchen, the sack-bag that formed the hearth
rug, the burnt potatoes and the corner under the stairs
– just like ours. And the bird's-nesting: Paul putting
his finger through the thorns into the round door of
a wren's nest. 'It's almost as if you were feeling inside
the live body of the bird . . . it's so warm.' And Paul
showing Miriam how the hen ate from his hand. 'He
started and laughed. "Rap, rap, rap!" went the bird's
beak in his palm.'

'That's all symbolic, you see,' said Martin. 'A parable,
really.'

'And Miriam's struggle with algebra,' I said. 'I know all about that!'

' "And when she showed him the roses splashing the darkness like stars . . . Point after point the steady roses shone out to them, seeming to kindle something in their souls. The dark came like smoke around, and still did not put the roses out . . . white, some curved and holy, others expanded in ecstasy." That's all metaphor, you see.'

'But Lawrence uses words like cowd and a tidy bit, meaning quite a lot – it's just like Little Ness!'

'I'm glad you like it,' Martin smiled. 'The stars are coming out. I'd best be off.'

I shut the fowl up, checked the gates and took the book to bed.

Little stars shone high up; little stars spread far away in the flood-waters, and firmament below. Everywhere the vastness and terror of the immense night which is roused and stirred for a brief while by day, but which returns and will remain at last eternally holding everything in its silence and its living gloom.

So Lawrence sang his mordant threnody, and I was lulled to sleep.

My body was growing fast and my mind was catching up. The Empty Room was my conservatoire. Aunt Alice's bookcase filled one wall. Another was occupied by the piano, Beethoven's sonatas, the Forty-Eight and every piece of music I heard on the wireless that could be obtained from Harris's music shop in the Square. I began to go to concerts. Moiseiwitsch came to the Walker Hall. I got there too early. He was practising in dim light. He growled at me like a bear. And I slunk out. Shrewsbury offered recitals and concerts –

not at the so-called Music Hall, which was given over to dancing – but at almost every other sizeable place, including – on Sundays – the Granada cinema. Choral and Orchestral Society concerts at the Allington Hall, Shrewsbury School, were conducted by our venerable Salopian, Frederic C. Morris, standing in profile to the audience for all to see the strength of his jaw, his aquiline nose, his admirable firm down-beat . . .

'Max Rostal, Franz Osborn, in the ballroom of the Lion Hotel, halfway up Wyle Cop. Both out of the top drawer!' said the lady sitting next to me after Jelly d'Aranyi's performance of Mozart's violin concerto no. 5 in A. 'You like the violin? . . . Starting tomorrow, all the Beethoven violin sonatas.'

The lady who wore a camel-hair coat had camel-coloured hair drawn up in a bun. She had penetrating Delft-blue eyes, a county voice and shining, natural smile. She was genuinely persuasive when she added, 'I'll get you in.'

'But there isn't a bus on Sunday,' I murmured, head down, keeping my voice low and trying not to say buz.

'We'll cycle. Yes? Where do you live?'

'Little Ness.'

'That's Nesscliff. I live at Wilcot. We'll meet at Great Ness turn. At two. Tomorrow.'

She disappeared in the emerging crowd. I made my way down the riverside path to the Raven Yard where the bus to Valeswood stood with steamed-up windows and almost as many people standing as there were in the seats. I kept getting off to allow more people to get on and to make sure that I stood by the door, the only source of fresh air.

'Top drawer . . . I'll get you in . . . We'll cycle . . . Yes? . . . Where do you live?' I was on top of the world. I had been taken up.

'You're going to the what?'

117

'The Lion ballroom.'

Hoots from Penny who still clung to the cowhouse door. Mother was charmed I'm sure, and had Sunday lunch ready early, after a struggle with the fire.

'Dickens used to stay there,' she said. 'But you make sure you're back in time to milk!'

I thought I was in the Palace of Versailles that afternoon. I had never seen such splendour; never heard such ravishing sonorities. Now Rostal rasped his violin, now plucked or stroked or tickled the strings. Now Osborn banged, now tantalized us, now toyed and dallied with a trill, now danced with mischievous delight. Their responses in the syncopated scherzo of the Spring sonata were quick-silver; their unanimity complete.

'There,' said the lady in the camel-hair coat, the sensible shoes and bun-drawn woolly hat. 'You enjoyed that, didn't you? See you again next week.'

And so, three Sundays running, I sat in the Adam ballroom, rose-pink, white and gold, while Rostal and Osborn took keys to top drawers and showered us with musical gold.

'*Messiah*, at Hanley . . . Suddaby, Jarred and Parry Jones – I've forgotten the bass. Norman Allin. The best in the business. I like a good bass!'

So to Hanley in the Potteries we took an early train. The lady in the camel-hair coat had got my ticket, and mocked my vain attempt to pay. 'You'll simply love *Messiah*. What singing there will be! "I know that my Redeemer liveth . . . " "Comfort ye . . . " '

The orchestra was ready, the choir in evening dress – all hushed and pieced together, as beautifully assembled as the shining chandelier.

'Sir Percy Hull – no, Dr Hull,' the lady whispered, rather loud. In came a white-haired, portly man in tails, tapped his music stand with his stick, coughed, and with slow booms and sudden twiddles, then overlapping

118

waves of sound he launched the Overture. 'Comfort ye,' the tenor sang, another portly man; then danced through 'Every valley'. And sat down.

'And the glory, the glory of the Lord,' the chorus shouted from the back, 'shall be, shall be . . . revealed. And all flesh shall see it . . . ' No one could have any doubt.

'For unto us a Child is born . . . ' Our certainties affirmed, bold Handel in his grand design brought forth the Prince of Peace. A hush of violins, a flute or two, then, silvery as a shepherd boy's pealed out the pure soprano of Elsie Suddaby.

'Rejoice, rejoice, rejoice a hundred times; a thousand Hallelujahs; King of Kings' – and everyone stood up.

The bass (and double bass) raged furiously together and told us of a mystery. The trumpet sounded and all was Blessing and Honour, Glory and Power and a thunderous Amen.

But best I loved the alto, gathering in the lambs. 'His arms,' she kept repeating, 'and ca-ar-ry-y them in His bosom . . . ' My mind was fixed on hers. 'And gent-ly lead those that are with young . . . '

Summertime was nearly over now. At home the lambs – those that were left – were nearly full grown. My mind went back to June: to short-lived lambs and even shorter-lived wild roses. How sad it is, I thought, that these most perfect creatures, symbols of purity and innocence, should fade or be destroyed so soon. And thinking of June, I thought of her: of Lisbet –

She was as sweet as a rose at the dawning
But somehow Fate hadn't meant her for me . . .

That word! I thought of the sun chasing the cloud

119

shadows over the hills. Do beauty and evanescence go always together?

I hoped I should see her again.

By Aladdin's Lamp

One of the Darbys' old retainers, Miss Want, was still at large in the village with a string of snuffly, laid-back Pekingese. She gave me an old book about the Passion Play at Oberammergau.

'We used to go regularly,' she said. 'Perhaps you will too, some day.' I didn't say I didn't think I would. The pictures were dark and unappealing and I didn't know what to make of the text. Martin said I would do better to read *A Glastonbury Romance*. But Martin was a Powys fanatic: J.C., T.F., *Mr Weston's Good Wine* and all.

I remember Oberammergau because I was earnestly trying to come to terms with it when Mother told me that the pig had come out in a diamond rash.

'A diamond rash?'

'Yes, red diamond shapes all over her back. You'd better ring for the vet.'

Installed in the post office kiosk, I remembered to press Button A.

Mr Sinclair answered at once. Again he was as good as his no-nonsense word.

121

'Swine erysipelas,' he said, giving the pig a jab; 'acute inflammation of the lymphatic vessels of the skin, caused by streptococcal infection. She'll be all rright in the morrnin'.' He took his clean, aseptic smell away and left me wishing I had kept my science up.

'So what was the matter with the pig?' Now Mrs Garry would never have asked me that. But Mrs Garry had gone and in her place had come a little wisp of a woman with red hard-worked hands, nut-cracker nose and chin. She wore a lap-around overall and a black beret permanently clapped over one eye.

'Swine erysipelas,' I said.

'Swine erysipelas, Dad,'. she telephoned the air and, turning to me, continued: 'He's out there somewhere reading some old book.'

'What are you reading?' I asked the seated figure by the yew tree that lent shelter to the post office's back door.

'*Seven Pillars of Wisdom.*' The words came with a puff of blue pipe-smoke from under a low-brimmed trilby hat. 'Lawrence, you know.'

'Oh, I like Lawrence,' I said, approaching eagerly.

'Your mother wants her cigarettes,' the black beret reminded me. 'Dad, don't stay out there too long. It's cold.'

Beneath the rain-stained trilby hat, the putty-coloured, fleshy face was quite unlined. The neck went deep into a khaki shirt and thickened as it went. The dull-brown coat and trousers thickened round the seat; the legs shrank into pulled-up khaki socks and smartly polished, stubby boots.

'Dad was a sergeant in the army, you know.' The putty-coloured finger stroked a putty-coloured lip on which was set a chopped moustache. You hardly noticed it. Not bristling much any more, I thought. But used to making others jump.

The quiet, pipe-occluded voice said, 'See.' The putty-coloured finger of a podgy hand – so obviously not accustomed to work – traced red and black lines on a map. 'Wadi Sirhan. Now back a bit, map two, you see the course he took from Akaba along the Hejaz railway to Damascus.' I saw the outline of the Red Sea; then, in greater detail, the Dead Sea, the River Jordan, Palestine, familiar still from maps at school at Little Ness.

'Oh, this is Lawrence of Arabia,' I said, too loud to hide my ignorance.

'Yes, 1917; the Arab Revolt.'

'Dad was in India,' the overall exclaimed.

'You'd like to read it? I'll lend it you. Here, come inside. I'm going in.'

I had never seen inside the house in Mrs Garry's time. That was where the 'wires' came through in technical obscurity; from here big Mr Garry was sent out in khaki smock and khaki puttees with a quarter staff in one hand, the telegram in the other, squinting, to pick his way through the village with Dinah, his little fox terrier, at his heels. He must have fought in the Boer War, Mr Garry.

The floor inside the house was cardinal red. There was a pillarbox red kind of recess, a curtained door and one long shelf of books.

'I belong to a book club, you see. *Goodbye to All That, The Memoirs of an Infantry Officer* – take what you like.' I took all three.

And, by Aladdin's lamp that night, I went with Lawrence fixing gun-cotton and gelignite charges to the railway line; cutting telegraph wires and fastening the free ends to the saddles of the camels of rival tribesmen; rejoicing in the havoc he had made. We found the green oasis of El Kurr and there lay still, and received into our minds 'the sense of peace, the greenness and the presence of water which made this garden in the desert beautiful and haunting, as though previsited'.

The physical brilliance of Lawrence's writing evoked

all those biblical journeys previsited, yes, and learned by heart by me, a boy of ten, at school.

'What are you glued to now?' my mother asked.

'Lawrence of Arabia.' I unglued myself and glowed.

'A little tin god,' she scoffed. 'A mixed-up man.'

'A little tin man, maybe,' I said. 'But a mixed-up god!'

On my returning the *Memoirs* the putty sergeant told me he had seen Siegfried Sassoon throw his war-medals into the sea.

'At Southport,' said the overall. 'We lived there then.'

'Sassoon was quite sincere; but he could not keep away from the Front.' There was no mockery in the old man's voice.

I had only heard my father's tragic, tram-line version of the war. I did not even know where the Dardanelles were or to what an extent the Middle East had been involved.

'Did you think your father was only in France?' My mother left the question in the air.

Thus, people unlocked doors and closed them in your face. A window went up; a blind came down.

But I have always been grateful to those people who lent or gave me books: the sergeant with his noncommittal, smoke-occluded voice; Mrs Darby, who gave me *Pip, Squeak and Wilfred* when I was eight and the Book of Common Prayer when I was ten; Mrs Bowles who gave me *The Knapsack*, Herbert Read's pocket selection of poems for soldiers; our fine, selective parson who gave me not only *The Story of Little Ness* but also *The Fifth Form at St Dominic's*; and even Miss Want and her book of Oberammergau.

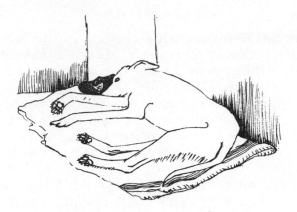

Summer's End

In addition to books, I had my daily letters to read: letters from all my Priory friends, but chiefly from Lisbet who had the franchise of the moonbeams. Maurice, who was now at Oxford, wrote almost as often. His letters were all about Jane Austen, *Beowulf* and the OUDS. Had I read James Agate's *Ego* books? He was on number eight. Had I heard the Jupiter? What did I do all the time?

And then it came. It came in a buff envelope: OHMS.

'It's from the War Office.'

'It's your call-up papers.'

'What shall I do?'

'You'll have to send them back.'

'What? Tell them I can't come?'

'The cows won't milk themselves.' My mother knew what to say.

'The cows won't milk themselves,' I wrote. But then I had a better idea. I put my half-baked letter with the papers in the envelope.

'I'll go and see the War Ag. lot.'

'Yes, go and see Captain Pullman.'

125

Captain Pullman was the chairman of the War Agricultural Executive Committee. He was known as a man who got things done. I knew him only by sight: a lean, ascetic man in a deer-stalker, Norfolk jacket, breeches and leggings. He carried a cane and still issued army-style commands, slapping the cane on the hard casing of his calf. I would go and see Captain Pullman. Not at his office in town: at his country house in Wilcot, I thought.

Would he be on the side of the farmer or that of the army, I wondered, as I bumped along on my buckle-wheeled bike. I put my hand in my inside pocket to check that the envelope was still there; and my mother's impromptu gambit – more of a gamble, I thought – 'the cows won't milk themselves'.

It was one of those mornings when you ride on air; bright with the bite of autumn. Late campion, vetch and toadflax; poppies and the secondary spires of foxgloves hugged the hedgerows and, higher up, a few small antlers still protruded from the honeysuckle's knobbly heads.

Wilcot was on the way to Pentre where I used to go to swap bantams for fantails with my old friend Davy Jones. It was also on the way to the army training grounds. Beyond them lay the Breidden with its finger-like pillar out there to the west. There were the scars of the quarry from which the famous Criggion green roadstone came. There too was Moel y Golfa with the Chell monument where an old Romany's ashes were strewn. There was Melverley with its foundations in the river, the alluvial fields where farmers pastured their cattle in spring, where in floodtime the horses stood neck-deep in water and hay was carried out to them in boats. There was the black and white church whose tarred timbers were caulked like a ship's, that stood no nonsense from hell or high water. OHMS – I flew!

I had only a rough idea where Captain Pullman

lived: some old baronial hall with wrought-iron gates and hunters in the paddock and Dobermann Pinschers padding about on trim and weedless lawns. Would he be in? He was a farmer, I thought. He didn't spend all his time at the War Ag. in town.

In Wilcot I saw the postman who told me where the Captain lived.

'A good bit yonder, it's a tidy way, but yo canna miss it. I tell ya what, I seed Mrs Pullman cuttin' down the 'erbaceous theer, not 'alf a 'our ago. Yo looken out fer 'er!'

I thanked him and bumped on. My crank protested every time I turned the pedal round. The cotter-pin was loose and my right foot slipped from twelve o'clock to two with no effect. If this goes on, I thought, I'll walk. It was embarrassing.

Just then I saw the lady in the camel-hair coat. Apart from the gardening gloves and secateurs, the ensemble was the same; the same sensible shoes and the bun-drawn woolly hat.

'Ah, I've just got tickets for *Elijah* . . . Harvey Alan at St Chad's. You'll come?'

'Of course,' I said. 'That's if I'm here.' I asked where Captain Pullman lived.

'Why, here, of course. Didn't you know?'

By now I did. He stood there in his deer-stalker tapping his buskins with his cane. No Dobermann Pinscher padded up, but a soft-mouthed yellow Labrador who wanted, it seemed, to read my letter first.

'Dead, Sandy,' came the Captain's voice, and Sandy sat, well-drilled but laughing in a friendly way while I half-dropped my bike and ummed and erred and fumbled with the envelope.

'OHMS! Oh dear, but don't worry. Leave it with us.' The lady in the camel-hair coat took charge.

'Yes, yes,' the Captain volunteered. 'We'll see to it.'

'He'll get you awf! You'd like a drink, I expect?'

'No thanks, I'm on my way to Melverley.'

'Awl right . . . St Chad's, on Saturday . . . The round church on Town Walls. At seven o'clock!'

I picked up my bike off the road and pedalled on to Melverley; a hiccup with each grinding revolution of my crank. A song came back to me from many years before:

> You won't see any big parade,
> There won't be any bugle played,
> Sad to say no war today
> 'Cos the General's fast asleep . . .
> The Colonel's mad and the Major's blue,
> The Captain's sad and the Sergeant too,
> Guess this war will have to keep,
> It's enough to make an army weep . . .

Another of the songs my mother brought back from town on a Saturday night.

'Where've you been?' my mother asked when I reached home. She was standing at the iron gate, the one that separated the farmyard from the little yard at the side of the house. This was the gate that clanked every time the postman, the butcher, the baker or the oilman came through. It sounded a warning note. It ensured that Mother was ready when they arrived at the door. But Mother must have heard the fold gate shut – or, possibly, the knocks that issued from my worn-out bike.

'You won't look so pleased with yourself when you see the poor old dog,' she said. The relief at not being called up must have shown on my face.

'What's happened?' I asked.

'Nothing – and that's the worry.' She frowned. 'Penny's watching over him.'

We went inside the house where Gyp lay panting on the hearth. Penny was sitting on the settle, leaning over him and comforting him, her long-fingered hand on his attenuated frame.

'He's panting, but he's cold,' she said. 'Poor boy!'

'You'd better call the vet,' my mother said. 'He'll put him down.'

I tried to feel his pulse but nowhere, not in his chest or in his leg, could I get a response.

'Pneumonia will set in,' my mother exclaimed and gave me a push to the door. 'It would be a kindness to have him put to sleep.'

I did not stop to argue. We all knew Gyp had gone beyond the help of a vet – except this one last act of mercy, which I, in all my dealings with Mr Sinclair, had never had to ask him to perform.

I raced across the fields, the short cut to the kiosk in Church Lane. In those two minutes the whole of Gyp's life passed before my eyes: his playful puppyhood; his easy graduation to knowing right from wrong; his first rabbit; his first hare; his swift and silent movement through the grass; his subtle suppleness – what my brother John called 'supple-ty'; the high parabola he described when leaping over a fence; the way he free-wheeled up a hill . . .

'I'll come rright away. I'm just finishing my lunch.'

I did not have to explain. Mr Sinclair understood. He knew our animals.

But only I knew what this meant. It meant our last link with the Cliffe was gone. Gyp was all that was left of that free world of our childhood. Gyp had given new meaning to such well-worn words as 'running like the wind'. His ears like little handkerchiefs flowed back. His head and tail were still, the neck and loins accomplishing the swerve. Like a coiled spring, he did not run – he revolved.

But lately he had become stiff. His rippling muscles had fallen away. His haunches looked like a stocking when Mother thrust her hand in it and pressed with her knuckles to seek out the holes. He was all skin and bone. He only wanted to sleep.

It was a long time since he had caught a hare; since he had voyaged with us to the edge of his known world. He slid through the cracks of life like a ghost. He lay like a shadow on the ground. Always a delicate eater, he had no appetite now. The wind was going out of him.

He looked at me when I returned, as if he knew that something was afoot. Penny had placed her old school hat, a brown velour, as a pillow for his head. Bending down to comfort him, I noticed the words on the badge in front. '*Semper Fidelis*,' I read aloud, and let a tear roll down on Gyp.

We sat about, my mother, Penny and I. We did not fancy eating lunch.

'I'll make another pot of tea,' my mother said, and smiled a misty smile.

Behind our cups we kept our thoughts to ourselves, out of respect for the always quiet Gyp. I tried to think what my last words to him might be. (He never 'yowked'.) Where would I bury him?

The vet came whistling in. The women withdrew a little to one side.

'Can ye rraise a vein forr me,' he asked. I held Gyp's foreleg gingerly and tried to say 'Shake hands!'

'Therr, therr!' The vet could spot the vein. He gently dabbed the leg with disinfected lint and slipped the needle in, then dabbed it with the lint again. 'He'll be all rright. I'll take him with me then?'

'Oh, will you? Good,' my mother said.

Vet and knackerman combined, I thought – but the words stuck in my throat. 'I'll help you carry him,' I volunteered.

I took Gyp in my arms. He looked at me, as if to register his thanks.

'He was always a quiet dog,' I told the vet.

130

'The best thing ye can say of any dog,' he smiled.

We laid Gyp in the car. Penny did not want her old hat back.

'*Semper fidelis*,' I said and smiled at her.

Three quick revs and a *rhummm!* and Gyp was on his way to eternity.

'He's joined the travellers again,' I said to Penny.

'You get your lunch – and look after your mum,' she said sensibly, charging away on her well-oiled bike.

All Change at Little Ness

I carried on the farm in the same old way. It is easy to get in an agricultural rut. The years go by: spring, summer, harvest, winter . . . Spring brings hope of better times to come. Summer leads to harvest and the prospect of well-being you know the winter will destroy. But you carry on.

I did everything the hard way; milking by hand, by the light of a hurricane lamp as the nights grew long and cold: milking, foddering, mucking out . . . It was so cold sometimes I put a straw jacket round the pump; then set fire to it in the morning to thaw it out.

'This is the limit,' said John, as we broke the ice on the pit for the cows to get a drink. He was home for a whole week. The thirsty beasts slurped greedily from holes between sealed chunks of ice and tested it with hooves that creaked in answer to the ice. 'Everyone else has water and electricity laid on.' He whacked the ice with the axe and sent sharp, glassy slivers showering in my face.

'You split my head open with that axe,' I recalled, 'when we were small.'

'You stood too close,' he chimed. 'Stand back, and you won't get hurt.'

'I've still got the mark.'

'You carry your memories in your head.'

'And my chains around my feet,' I moped.

I read socially grey novels like *The Hole in the Wall* and *The Ragged Trousered Philanthropists*. I missed out on Orwell and made myself moody with Eliot and Pound.

Mother still got a solid pile of Francis Brett Youngs and Howard Springs from the library but was finding Agatha Christie easier to hold in bed. She reread Mark Twain. I could hear her cough, and sometimes laugh, and I could smell the smoke of candle and cigarette.

Aunt Alice came with her new companion and bosom friend, Miss Steele, whom she called Pet. Mother wondered what her real name was; I suggested Stainless. Mother told me to mind my Ns and Ms – 'What is your name? N or M?' I could not catechize her thus: to ask a lady's name was as bad as asking her age.

There were things you could not ask, and things you dared not tell.

Belle wrote from Lossiemouth to say she'd stripped an aircraft engine down. A Miles Master had crashed in the Cairngorms in fog. And she'd been out with Gilbert who was an Australian, an officer and very nice. In the next letter she said that Gilbert was married – the nice ones always were; she'd have to give him up. Life wasn't fair.

Laura was on the switchboard at Aldershot – whatever that meant. She was amazingly efficient, self-possessed and, unlike me, grown-up. She wore make-up, permed her hair, and grew her fingernails – except one, which she chewed, she said, when calls stopped coming in. She liked to hear me play 'So Deep is the Night' when she came home.

We had a wind-up gramophone on which we played 'Three Ha'pence a Foot', 'God Shall Wipe Away All Tears from Their Eyes' and the Serenade from *The Fair*

133

Maid of Perth. When we ran out of fibre needles, or the sharpener didn't work, we used a hawthorn from the hedge. We went to bed by candlelight, our shadows bulking on the stairway walls little bigger than they bulked when we were small. We woke to the same hard water, merciless cobblestones and garget in the milk. My sisters sighed like my mother for a house with a tap.

Laura, back at Aldershot, wrote to say that she was thinking of going to Canada. She could get a job as a stenographer. Her typing speed had gone up to sixty words a minute and her shorthand was 'OK'. Belle wrote from Lossiemouth: 'We've got a new Sea Fury – 2,500 hp. Home for Hogmanay. May Doth and Nicky come?'

Nicky Garland and Dorothy Clare had a repertoire of shaggy dog stories that spurted round our hearth like naughty jumping jacks and kept us entertained while Robert Donat droned through *In Memoriam* and 1948 crept in. Nicky, seated on the floor in a water-silk blouse and flared, plaid skirt, her stockinged feet tucked under it, looked like a Scottish Little Mermaid. Chestnuts exploded in the open fire. Nut-crackers cracked; and so long as we plied her with nuts, she kept up a steady stream of salty jokes. A natural entertainer, she might have ended up at Drury Lane. 'Should auld acquaintance be forgot . . . '

In those years of regulation comings and goings Little Ness had become a staging post for travellers nation-wide: Laura holding the line at Aldershot; Martin, an education officer in Lincolnshire; Kite at Catterick, still reportedly cleaning out latrines; Dickie with the RAF at Bridgnorth, Maurice at Oxford; and my brother still tinkering with radar in the distant Malvern hills . . . But Martin was soon to go to Turkey, Kite to Hong Kong, Dickie to Rhodesia, and my brother and sister Laura to Canada.

I was going to be a student at the Guildhall School of Music in London. I had been accepted. I hardly knew how.

Hard and cold was the rest of that winter; cold and empty was the spring. Things long considered, long put off, long talked about and long dismissed, came swiftly in the end and overtook us, almost unawares.

Mother instructed her solicitors, Messrs Beale & Burr, to deal with the sale. Mr Blithe with billycock hat, bow legs and bright bow-tie would sell the house and land, in Shrewsbury, on such and such a day at three o'clock. Three weeks later the 'effects', the desirable dairy cows, poultry, implements, fodder, etc., would be auctioned on the premises. All of which we viewed with dread.

Mr Beale, in black city coat and startling yellow wig, saw the dear house knocked down to the farmer who lived next door. It was dear to us and cheap to him. Mr Blithe found us a bijou house in town which cost, I think, about the same. Still, Mother didn't mind – for all her married life she'd wanted a house with a tap, and this had all mod. cons.

Why didn't we go to the sale? 'It's like going to a funeral,' my mother said, and none of us went to funerals.

But the dispersal sale was another matter. You can live in your house temporarily after it has been sold and still pretend that nothing has changed; but when the auctioneer mounts the boards and knocks down all your favourite stock in numbered lots – stock that it has taken twenty years to build – he knocks them down to alien hands. He sells them coop by coop and stall by emptied stall. They are hustled and driven, heads down, from the scene.

'Stand back; let's see her walk around.' Your favourite Friesian Anna, bagged up for the occasion, docile in a halter, is led with unfamiliar pomp around the yard that's been her freehold all her life.

'Goin' at twenty-eight ten, gentlemen . . . For the last time, twen'y-eight poun' ten – *bang!*'

You turn your head away because you cannot bear to see her shuffled off and mounted onto a lorry, her milk squirting from her teats, her hind legs strained about a yard apart.

You see again the empty poultry pens and hear the cheeping of the chicks that perhaps you helped break into the world. (I sometimes helped them from their dark, impenetrable shells.) Imagination plays strange tricks: there are no chicks – but one old bantam cockerel flies up to a wall, he flaps his wings and crows – the last free-booter running free.

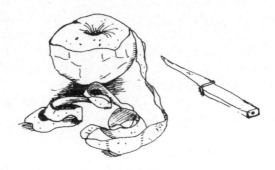